My Sweet Savior

90 Day Devotional

Building an Intimate Relationship with Jesus

Armani D. White

My Sweet Savior

90 Day Devotional

Building an Intimate Relationship with Jesus

Copyright Page

'My Sweet Savior — Building an intimate Relationship with Jesus — 90 Day Devotional'
Written by Armani White

Copyright © 2020 by Armani White.
All Rights Reserved.

Published by: Rise Ministry, Inc.'s Publishing Group
ISBN: 978-1-7351105-1-6
Printed in the United States of America.

All rights reserved. No part of this publication may be reproduced, stored in a retrieval system, or transmitted in any form or by any means – electronic, mechanical, photocopy, recording, scanning or otherwise – without the prior written consent of the publisher, except by provided by the United States of America copyright law. Scripture quotations are taken from the New King James Version®. ©1982 by Thomas Nelson. Used by permission.

Forwarded by: Elder Veronica Spight

Cover Design: Armani White

Table of Contents

Dedication vii

Foreword viii

Introduction ix

Love 11

Joy 25

Peace 39

Longsuffering 53

Kindness 67

Goodness 81

Faithfulness 95

Gentleness 109

Self-Control 123

   Closing 139

   Ending Prayer 141

   Salvation Prayer 143

Dedication

To the woman who desires to mature and grow in her walk. Know that I am always praying for you and rooting for you. You got this sis, hang in there. Jesus loves you always and forever!

Foreword

Oh, taste and see that the Lord is good; Blessed is the man who trusts in Him! – Psalms 34:8

౭౩

    We desire to have a deeper relationship with the Lord and walk uprightly before Him. At some point, most of us struggle with the questions of "am I living my best life?" or "am I honoring the Lord with all that I am?". I believe these questions are part of the growing process as we develop a closer relationship with the Lord.

    As we learn to trust His love for us, we know in our spirit that God loves us, and His love for us will never fail. The **B**ible says in 1 John 4:16, "And we have known and believed the love that God has for us. God is love, and he who abides in love abides in God, and God in him."

    "My Sweet Savior" pours out the love of God towards us. This 90-day devotional illustrates God's love for us in the fruits of the spirit of love, joy, peace, patience, kindness, goodness, faithfulness, gentleness, and self-control. The pages of this lovely 90-day devotional are drenched in the spirit of the Lord! This is an Amazing devotional and clearly inspired by the spirit of God.

    This 90-day devotional intimately and lovingly helps us to reflect on God's love and purpose for our lives. It is a great ministry tool for the un-saved, church groups, friends, and family.

Forwarded by
Elder Veronica Spight
Covenant Life Church – VA

Introduction

There she stood, in the middle of the room, completely naked and vulnerable. As she stood clenching her oil filled jar, she debated whether she should approach Him. She feared that if she went any closer, those who knew of her past would mock, tease, and even shame her. She also questioned if HE would receive her. *What would stop Him from rejecting her like everyone else?* Yet, slowly, she approached, bringing forth one foot in front of the other, weeping, full of tears and sorrow as the weight of her sins weighed her down.

After what seemed like eons, she finally reached the altar. She fell on her knees, feeling naked, venerable, and unsure if she should surrender or hold on to what she knew. But then she heard, "Mary." Upon hearing the sweet voice of her Savior calling her name, both hands rose in submission. She forgot about her oil and everyone in the room. But they didn't forget about her. They shamed her for dropping and breaking her jar of oil at the feet of Jesus. But her Christ silenced their shame by calling her even closer.

Recognizing that Mary had spilled and broken her jar of oil, He gave her a new vessel with more oil. Jesus traded her pain for purpose; Her shame for confidence; Her sorrow for laughter; Her sadness for gladness. He even gave her an influx of what she never had, such as love, joy, peace, endurance, kindness, goodness, faithfulness, gentleness, and self-control. Her Savior Redeemed her.

Finally, Mary raises herself in a hurry. She noticed her oil spilling on her. When she looked, her jaw dropped as she was surprised at what she saw. A new vessel beautifully adorned with gold around the rim and flowers dressing the glass. She continued to watch in amazement as she saw that the oil in the vessel was never-ending and overflowing. She said to herself, 'surely, my cup runs over.'

As Mary was turning away to leave the altar, Jesus spoke to her telling her, her life from that day on will never be the same. For she had been saved, redeem, and made whole. He also gave her fruit for her Journey. Her fruit had the scriptures Galatians 5:22-25 written on it. Finally, Jesus kissed and gave her another embrace as He said, 'My Spirit is forever with you. Listen to My voice, for I am always here.'

ಶ‍ಲ

My prayer for you as you embark on this 90-day devotional is that you surrender everything at the feet of Jesus like the woman in Luke 7:37. During this time, we're going to take a closer look at Jesus and His fruit as outlined in the Bible. It is my earnest belief that as a believer and follower of Jesus Christ, we are to bear His fruit while building an intimate relationship with Him. After all, He said, "If we live in the Spirit (His Spirit), let us walk in the Spirit (His Spirit)." – Galatians 5:25 Amen.

Love

My Sweet Savior • 90 Day Devotional

His Love *Day 1*

"For God so loved the world that He gave His only begotten Son, that whoever believes in Him should not perish but have everlasting life. For God did not send His Son into the world to condemn the world, but that the world through Him might be saved." – John 3:16-17

☙

God's Words are forever true. John 3:16-17 tells us that His love for us is so great that He gave His ONLY Son as a sacrifice for us. The only key is to **believe**. If you believe that God sent His only Son, Jesus, to die for you and rose from the grave so that you will be saved, then by faith you'll have everlasting life through Christ, Jesus.

When you are redeemed, God no longer looks at the sins of your past. Scriptures like Isaiah 43:25, tells us that God wipes away your sins. He remembers them no more. In fact, He considers you a new creation, because, through Christ, you have a fresh start. In Christ, you are renewed.

As you reflect on today, remember how God gave you a new start at life. Your new life started when God sent His only Son to die for your sins and when He decided to forgive your debt.

Dear Heavenly Father

Thank You for saving and cleansing me of my sins. Lord, I ask that You continue to remind me that in You, I am a new creation. In Jesus' name, I pray, amen.

NOTE: If you've never given your life to Christ and would like to do so, please read our Salvation Prayer that's located in the back of this Devotional.

Love

Day 2

A Father's Love

"A Father of the fatherless, a defender of widows, is God in His holy habitation. God sets the solitary in families; He brings out those who are bound into prosperity, but the rebellious dwell in a dry land." - Psalm 68:5-6

ೞ

One of many things about God is that HE LOVES His children. God loves you so dearly. I'm not sure where you are right now in your walk and life. But God wants you to know that He loves you. Many people may have hurt you. You may have experienced an influx of people in and out of your life. However, such is not so with God.

God will never leave you nor forsake you. He is a Father who will NEVER abandon His children. Sure, there are moments where it appears as if God is absent. However, if you incline your ears to the still, sweet voice of the Holy Spirit, you'll notice that He is forever present even in your darkest and quietest moments.

Your Father Loves you, and He is waiting for you to surrender your heart to Him. He desires to build a more intimate relationship with you. But this will require trust and vulnerability.

As you continue your day, remember that the Lord loves you, and He thinks good thoughts towards you.

Dear Heavenly Father

Thank You for loving me unconditionally. Thank You for being a Father, Friend, and forever present in my life. Lord, help me to acknowledge You in all my ways. In Jesus' name, I pray, amen.

Day 3
I surrender

"Trust in the Lord with all your heart, and lean not on your own understanding; In all your ways acknowledge Him, and He shall direct your paths" - Proverbs 3:5-6

☙

God's ultimate will for our lives is to surrender to Him. The act of surrendering is to release complete and total control to the Savior, Jesus Christ. However, surrendering requires trust. It takes faith, knowing that God is a Good Father, and He will lead you in a clear path. It takes trust knowing that His way far outweighs yours. It takes trust in God to surrender your mindsets, desires, and ideas into the hands of the Father and allow Him to lead you in your purpose.

Today, remember that God is a good Father, know that there is nothing that surprises God. Therefore, cling to Him as He leads you.

Dear Heavenly Father

Help me to acknowledge You in all my ways. Help me to understand that You are for me and not against me. Help me to realize that You will lead in a clear path. And Father, help me to trust You in all things. In Jesus' name, I pray, amen.

Love

Day 4

He Loves, So I can

"A new commandment I give to you, that you love one another; as I have loved you, that you also love one another" – John 13:34

ଔ

Christ came so that we can have life through Him. Aside from that, He came so that we can live as He lived. Living as Christ lived, will require us to love as He loves. However, let's be honest. Loving our family and friends can be challenging. There are things they do and habits they have that drive us crazy, thus making it harder to love them.

Well, this is the same way God looks at us. The only difference is that He looks beyond our flaws and chooses to love us. Love is a choice; therefore, you may not feel like loving someone, but despite their flaws and hang-ups, you can still choose to love them.

Today, challenge yourself to love those who make it hard for you to love them. Go beyond the perception of how love is supposed to look and feel. Choose to love despite what you see.

Dear Heavenly Father

In Jesus' name, Lord, I ask that You help me to walk in the grace of love. Help me to understand that Love is a choice, and I have the strength and power through Jesus Christ to love those who You've placed in my path. In Jesus' name, thank You, for giving me the grace to Love. Amen.

I am Precious

Day 5

"Keep me at the apple of Your eye; hide me under the shadow of Your wings." – Psalm 17:8

☙

The Psalmist David prayed a bold and powerful prayer; He declared that he is the apple of God's eye. David knew that God checked his motives and his heart, time and time again. Yet, regardless of all the adversities, God still found him a man after His own Heart. Knowing this, David knew that God favored Him because, in all seasons, his heart was aligned with God's will.

There comes a time, when despite your adversities, you will know that God still favors you. You'll see that you're favored because you would have stood the test of time and developed confidence in the Lord knowing that through all seasons, the good and the bad – God is still for you. Matter of fact, God considers you a precious gem, the apple of His eye.

This morning, remember that God favors you. Remember that despite your circumstances, God loves you, and He still considers you His child. You are the apple of His eye!

Dear Heavenly Father

Help me to recognize that I am a precious gem in Your eyes. Help me to walk in confidence, knowing that You still consider me Your daughter and Your child. Lord, I thank You for loving me. In Jesus' name, I pray, amen.

Love

Day 6

Respect and Honor

"Honor your father and your mother, that your days may be long upon the land which the Lord your God is giving you." – Exodus 20:12

☙

Our earthly parents are a representation of God's love and parental guidance here on earth. However, there are many cases where parents are not the best representation, due to human errors or unfortunate mishaps. Nevertheless, we are called to honor and love our parents. We respect our parents despite their human-like flaws and give grace and understanding along the way. As children of God, we are called to love, honor, and respect our parents, as this is the only commandment with a promise – long life.

Today, be intentional about loving your Father and your Mother. Make a conscious choice to look beyond their faults and learn to love them more than you did yesterday.

Dear Heavenly Father

Lord God, I ask that You help me to honor my parents like never before. Help me to recognize that they're Your children, and You have handpicked them as my parents to love and nurture me. Father, I thank You for showing me how to give grace and love as You would have me do. In Jesus' name, I pray, amen.

My Sweet Savior • 90 Day Devotional

Day 7

The Power of Love

"There is no fear in love; but perfect love casts out fear, because fear involves torment. But he who fears has not been made perfect in love."
– 1 John 4:18

ೂ

The Love of God is the power that bring freedom and victory. In Christ, you don't have to be bound by torments. Trust that God's hands are long enough and powerful enough to save, free, and redeem you from all your struggles, torments, and suffering. Simply ask the Lord to free you. Believe in faith, knowing that God has the power to bind and cast out all torments and pain.

Today, choose not to struggle in silence. Ask the Lord to save you from whatever is keeping you bound. Ask the Lord to align your steps with the steps of those whom He has positioned to help you and minister to you. God cares about your heart and your wellbeing. He desires to see you walk in your true freedom.

Dear Heavenly Father

Lord, I ask that You lead me on the path of complete and total healing. Lord, I want to be free from all torments and pains that are keeping me bound. Father, I trust and believe that You've set me free in Jesus' name. Amen.

Love

Day 8

Transformative Love

"And above all things have fervent love for one another, for love will cover a multitude of sins." – 1 Peter 4:8

☙

There may be many people in your circle, people you know, who are still struggling with sin. Perhaps, you may even be that person who's struggling. Luckily, the Lord tells us that love covers a multitude of sins. Which means that we are charged with loving others, despite the appearance of sin. The love we show others – without judgment – is what will lead them to true salvation through Christ Jesus.

As you continue your day, remember that the only power that can save is the Love and power of Christ. It is only through Christ where one can be freed and saved from sins and iniquity.

Dear Heavenly Father

Lord, I ask that You help me to be a light in dark places. Help me to show the love of Christ, so that others can experience Your true love and salvation. In Your Holy Son, Jesus' name I pray, amen.

Day 9

Ultimate Love

"And now abide faith, hope, love, these three; but the greatest of these *is* love." – 1 Corinthians 13:13

☙

There are many stipulations, 'laws' and commandments that are listed in the Bible. However, God ultimately charges us with Love. He charges us to walk and live in love, because our motives are pure only through true, authentic, genuine, and Christ-like love. Everything we do will either be driven by Christ's love or worldly passions. Therefore, let love be your ultimate desire.

Today, I want to charge you with being intentional about checking your motives and being mindful of walking in the Love of Christ. As you go about your day, ask yourself: Am I being driven by love, or are my motivations rooted in the world?

Dear Heavenly Father

Lord, I ask that You help me to walk in love in all that I do. Lord, purify my heart and strengthen my love for You, myself, and others. Father, I desire to walk in the love of Christ. In Jesus' name, I pray, amen.

Love

Day 10

Intentional

"Beloved, let us love one another, for love is of God; and everyone who loves is born of God and knows God." – 1 John 4:7

ଓ

God is love. For this reason, all who believe in Christ and accept Him as Lord and Savior, have the power and ability through Jesus to walk in love. Walking in love may not be an easy task; nevertheless, love is a fruit that was planted inside of your spirit the moment you committed your life to Christ.

Just like any other vegetation, the fruit of love takes cultivation. It requires you to be intentional about choosing to love others despite what you see. It also means that you depend on the Father to lead you in the Spirit of Love. It also takes trusting that God will never leave you nor forsake you and that He's walking with you through this journey called love. After all, God so loved the world that He gave His only begotten Son, and God loves the world so much that He desires to share His love to and through His creation. He wants to share His love through YOU!

Remain encouraged, knowing that God is doing good work in you. The Fruit of Love is already in you. As the Father continues to mold you in His image, you'll see more of the produce of love.

Dear Heavenly Father

Lord, I thank You for showing me Your love so that I may love myself and others as You have loved me. Father, I ask that You continue to strengthen me and show me how to love and give grace always. In Jesus' name, I pray, amen.

Words for You

God's ultimate desire for you is to love. He desires that you love Him with all your heart and be intentional about expressing and showing your love for Him. There's no right or wrong way to be intentional about spending some good ol' quality time with Jesus – just do it! This intentionality may be in the form of reading this devotional every morning, reading your Bible, going to church, praying, being in fellowship, or sitting in silence and listening.

Ultimately, you are walking as Proverbs 3:5-6 tells us to walk; you are acknowledging the Lord in all that you do; you consider and trust God's will; you know that He will direct your path according to the purposes that He set for you. In the beginning, you may not always see the direction in which God is leading you. However, as you spend time with the Holy Spirit, you'll grow to know the voice of God, and you'll develop trust in both yourself and in God knowing that you are capable of hearing from God and knowing that God will never leave you nor forsake you.

Dear Heavenly Father

Lord, I pray for Your daughter. Father, I pray that she will continue to grow to love You more. Father develop in Her, the spirit of determination as she continues this walk of faith. Lord, I pray that You bless her from the top of her crown to the soles of her feet. Father, I pray that You strengthen her heart as she shows the love of Christ to others. In Jesus' name, I pray, amen.

Quiet Time

Prayer Request

Reflective Notes	**Reflective Questions**

Scriptures

Joy

Day 11
Faith that produces Joy

"But without faith, *it is* impossible to please *Him,* for he who comes to God must believe that He is and *that* He is a rewarder of those who diligently seek Him." – Hebrews 11:6

☙

Life has a way of taking us into the storm. It places us in compromising situations and floods us with mixed emotions, all while challenging our ability to walk in the confidence that God is Lord over all.

Through your circumstances and experiences, God is molding and stretching you to build your faith in Him.

As your faith builds, joy is produced. Joy comes with knowing that despite your situations, whether good or bad, God is forever present and always in control. Joy says, 'despite what I see or feel, my faith is in the Lord, rather than what's in front of me.'

As you go about your day, remember you have a choice. Choose to walk in total joy, knowing that your faith is anchored in the Lord. As a result, your needs are fulfilled by the Father.

Dear Heavenly Father

Lord, I pray that You strengthen my faith and belief in You. Father, help me to understand that pure joy comes from You and not my circumstances. Lord, I thank You for strengthening Your Spirit of Joy within me. In Jesus' name, I pray, amen.

Joy

Day 12

The Joy of Restoration

"He shall pray to God, and He will delight in him, He shall see His face with joy, For He restores to man His righteousness." – Job 33:26

☙

God desires to restore you into right standing with Him. The Lord wants to wash you, cleanse you, and make you whole. The Lord is saying; no longer do you have to be subjected by sin, torment or death because I've come to give you an abundant life through Christ Jesus. I've come to provide you with joy as I restore you into the image of righteousness that I have destined for you. Come to ME, and I will heal you. I will restore your body, soul, and spirit. In Jesus' name.

As you increase your intentionality to build a deeper relationship with the Lord, know that you're in for complete and total restoration. The Lord will restore your spirit and birth new life within you. Trust that He is the only Father who brings complete and total healing, restoration, and Joy through Christ Jesus.

Dear Heavenly Father

Lord, I ask that You continue to work healing and restoration in me. Father, I delight in Your presence, and I thank You for restoring me in the image that You have for me. In Jesus' name, I pray, amen.

My Sweet Savior • 90 Day Devotional

Day 13

Rest Assured

"In the multitude of my anxieties within me, Your comforts delight my soul." – Psalm 94:19

ଔ

Just imagine, a Savior who cares about the total essence of who you are! Jesus cares so much for your soul that He died for every ounce of anxiety, fear, doubt, and uncertainty. He died so that you could be free in Him; free to love, free to live, and free to be whole.

The process of such freedom is often misunderstood. Freedom is not an independent journey; you have help in the Holy Spirit. Jesus sent His Spirit to be your helper, and to guide, direct, nurture, and usher you to your optimum freedom.

Joy comes from knowing that God will never leave you nor forsake you and that He has sent His Holy Spirit to be a present help in your time of need.

Sister, as you continue your walk of faith, remain in joy, knowing that God desires to set you free. Your freedom is through Jesus Christ as the Holy Spirit is here to comfort and help sustain you along the way.

Dear Heavenly Father

Father, help me to acknowledge Your Spirit every moment. Help me to know that You will never leave me nor forsake me. Lord, remind me that Your will is to heal me and to lead me to optimal joy. Father, I thank You for loving me. In Jesus' name, I pray, amen.

Joy

Day 14

Delight of Integrity

"It is a joy for the just to do justice, but destruction will come to the workers of iniquity." – Proverbs 21:15

ಃ

Often, it may appear as if your good deeds, your dedication, your faithfulness, and your contentment in the Lord are going unnoticed. However, it's not. Although people may not acknowledge your efforts of living a life for Christ, God does. The Lord sees all that you've done. God is proud of your faith and your desire to seek and please Him.

Rest assured, knowing that God delights in your integrity. He is a rewarder of those who diligently seek Him, and who are intentional about living their lives according to His will. Therefore, continue to strive towards living Christ-like. Your reward is stored up in Heaven.

At this moment, I want to encourage you to remain in faith and keep your eyes on the Lord. It will seem as if people are always passing you and overlooking you; however, God sees you. – Allow that to be your joy and hope.

Dear Heavenly Father

Lord, I ask that You help me keep my eyes on You. Father, I know that You delight in my integrity, faithfulness, and my desire to please You. Holy Spirit, I ask that You continue to strengthen me and keep me in full joy as I continue to walk purposefully in the Lord. In Jesus' name, Lord, I thank You, amen.

Day 15

Have you asked of Him?

"Until now, you have asked nothing in My name. Ask, and you will receive, that your joy may be full." - John 16:24

ଔ

Just like natural parents who give you according to your needs and even when you ask, they're diligent with giving you the desires of your heart - the Lord is the same way. As a child of God who is seeking the Lord, it's okay to ask according to your desires. If your motives and intentions are pure and your dreams are to please God and not of selfish ambitions, then have joy knowing that as a child of God, the Lord will fulfill the desires of your heart.

Today, be confident in this, God looked into your heart. He heard your cry. He listened to your prayers. God knows of all that you need and want. At this present moment, God is preparing and molding you to be able to receive and sustain all that he has in store for you. Rest in joy, knowing this truth.

Dear Heavenly Father

Lord, I thank You for hearing my prayers, cries, and concerns. Father, I thank You for being a Faithful Father and for giving me the desires of my heart. Lord, I know that as I seek You, Your desires will become my desires. So, Father, I thank You for giving me a heart that is ready to please You. In Jesus' name, I pray, amen.

Joy

Day 16

Rejoice Always

"But let all those rejoice who put their trust in You; Let them ever shout for joy, because You defend them; Let those also who love Your name Be joyful in You." – Psalm 5:11

☙

As a child of God, you have this blessed hope that God is for you. He is a good Father who cares for His children. God desires to tend to your every need. He wants to transform your heart into healing and complete restoration in Him. Remain in full joy, keeping total trust in the Lord, knowing that God is for you and not against you.

This morning, continue to rejoice, even during setbacks and adversities. Know that all that you've been through is preparing you for the greater reality that God has for you. Walk in the Joy of the Lord, knowing that He has the final say, and His will far outweighs the bad.

Dear Heavenly Father

Lord, I ask that You fill me with the Joy of Your Spirit knowing that You are a good Father and that You delight in me. Father, remind me of this truth as I strive to live a life dedicated to You. In Jesus' name, I pray, amen.

My Sweet Savior • 90 Day Devotional

Day 17

Straight and Narrow

"You will show me the path of life; In Your presence *is* fullness of joy; At Your right hand *are* pleasures forevermore." – Psalm 16:11

☙

The moment you dedicated your life to Christ was the moment you became a co-heir to His Kingdom. As a co-heir of God's Kingdom, you have full access to life in eternity. The path towards eternity is very scantily traveled, but it is attainable.

The Lord gives us clear instructions in His Word – The Holy Bible – on how we should walk as co-heirs destined for eternity. That is, to honor and believe in the Lord Jesus Christ and to submit our ways to Him, thus, leading you to the fullness of joy that leads to a full life in Christ.

As you dedicate yourself to living a life for Jesus, He'll direct your ways according to His glory. In due season, you'll begin to notice a progression in your walk, behavior, and desires. This progressive change should be more inclined in the direction of how God sees you and the will He has destined for you. As an encouragement, stay the course and enjoy every moment of your walk.

Dear Heavenly Father

Lord, I thank You for guiding and leading me in Your will. Father, I ask that You keep my feet from falling. Holy Spirit, I ask that You strengthen me and bring all of God's Word to remembrance. Lord, cover me and embrace me in Your glory for Your name's sake. In Jesus' name, I pray, amen.

Joy

Day 18

Restore to me the Joy of the Lord

"Restore to me the joy of Your salvation, and uphold me *by Your* generous Spirit." – Psalm 51:12

☙

If I can be honest for a moment, there are times where we as Children of God, forget that there's joy in salvation. At times, life may sap any evidence of Joy that's within us. Sadly, this happens to a lot of us. Thankfully, this feeling and this season of hopeless and sleepless nights has an end.

The Lord's Word in Psalm 30:5 tells us that Joy comes in the morning. Joy comes when you realize and make it up in your mind that the pain and heartache you're feeling today will not dictate or justify your tomorrow. Instead, you will share in the glory of the Lord and walk in your God-given freedom of pure Joy and the Love of Life.

Walking in the Joy of the Lord is not easy. Luckily, it's a fruit of the Spirit. Joy being a fruit means that you have the ability and authority to nurture, pursue, and cultivate the Spirit of Joy that the Lord has given you. Choose today to be intentional about walking in Joy. Let no one nor anything rob you of your God-given Joy!

Dear Heavenly Father

Lord, I understand that I have the power and ability to walk in the full joy that You've given me. Father, I ask that You help and teach me to walk in that Joy for Your namesake. In Jesus' name, I pray, amen.

My Sweet Savior • 90 Day Devotional

Day 19

Joy that Heals

"Let us come before His presence with thanksgiving; Let us shout joyfully to Him with psalms." – Psalm 95:2

☙

There will come a day in your life where you will wake up and gracefully thank God for everything that has ever occurred in your life. Whether good or bad, in hardship or prosperity, you'll thank God for it all. The moment when you reach an understanding of healing, will be the moment when you can honestly and wholeheartedly give thanks to God for all that has ever come your way. True healing and revelation in the Lord's goodness creates pure joy. It also creates a love for what the Lord is and has been doing in your life.

Many people seek after happiness; however, happiness is temporal. When things are not happening as you wish, happiness fades. Instead of striving towards happiness and looking for substances that will give you instant gratification, look towards the Lord for Joy. Joy comes when you can see the goodness in your life, whether you're in a good or not so good season. Choose today to walk in the Joy of the Lord.

Dear Heavenly Father

Lord God, I ask that You continue to do the work of Joy in my life. Father, I thank You for showing me that pure joy comes from You. Thank You for loving me and pouring Your oil into my life, so that I can feel and live the joy that You've given. In Jesus' name, I pray, amen.

Joy

Day 20

God's Delight

"I have no greater joy than to hear that my children walk in truth." - 3 John 1:4

☙

To know the Father's heart is to know God's will. Scriptures like 2 Peter 3:9 and 1 Timothy 2:4 tells us that God's will is that no man shall perish but rather come into the knowledge that God yearns for us to repent, love, and acknowledge Jesus Christ as our Savior. God loves you. Therefore, He wishes for you to turn from your old ways and say YES to Jesus. This rededication and walking in the truth of life gives God joy.

Just like a natural father finds joy when his children are in the safety of his presence, so does our Heavenly Father. God's desire is for all His children to make their way into His arms of safety. It doesn't matter how long it takes you; all that matters is that you say Yes to Jesus and follow Him. If you have yet to commit your life to Christ, I want to encourage you to do so. If you need help in this process, feel free to reach out to the Rise Ministry, Inc.'s team - we'll help walk you through. You can visit: www.RiseMinistry.org/RomansRoad also, please see our Salvation Prayer at the end of this Devotional

Dear Heavenly Father

Lord, I thank You for choosing to save me from the pit of Hell. Lord, I thank You for seeing me as more than enough and for having the joy and desire to show me Your truth and the will of Your heart. Father, I love You and thank You for saving me. In Jesus' name, I pray, amen.

Words for You

Psalm 30:5 tells us that "Weeping may endure for a night, But joy comes in the morning." Joy comes when you can see that your weeping, your sorrow, your heartache, and your troubles are all purposeful. It's never God's intention to harm nor hurt you. However, some roads are a bit rockier than others; therefore, God chooses to use your journey.

The moment you dedicated your life to Christ, you gave God permission to use everything. Your entire life's journey will be used for the glory of God and your good. Your experiences are now life lessons, and your roadblocks have now transformed into steppingstones. Most importantly, your past is what is anchoring you for a higher purpose in Christ.

The moment you choose to see the beauty of God's glory in all situations, you will wake up and realize that God's joy surpasses all your pain.

Dear Heavenly Father

Lord, I pray that my sister in Christ will walk in her full God-given joy. Father, I pray that she sees herself in Your image and realize that You love her. Lord, we also know that Your desire for her is to walk in the complete freedom of Your joy. So, in faith she will walk in Your Joy. In Jesus' name, I pray, amen.

Quiet Time

Prayer Request

Reflective Notes | **Reflective Questions**

Scriptures

Peace

Day 21

Pursue Godly Peace

"And the peace of God, which surpasses all understanding, will guard your hearts and minds through Christ Jesus." – Philippians 4:7

ଓଃ

God's peace is unlike the world's peace. The Lord's peace gives you assurance, confidence, and sustainability to faithfully and boldly walk in the path of God. God's peace surpasses human understanding. God's peace is unfathomable, yet attainable. God's peace is having that sure, godly confidence in your spirit, knowing that God loves you and that He is in control.

The Peace of God confirms everything that He has spoken over your life.

The world's 'peace' can leave you with a false sense of confidence. It causes you to trust what your eyes can see and what you can readily reach. However, this type of peace can leave you feeling anxious, confused, and full of doubt. Therefore, at all costs, pursue the peace of the Lord. The Lord's peace is the one true peace which brings forth life and hopes through Jesus Christ.

Dear Heavenly Father

Lord, I thank You for giving me Your fruit of peace. Father, I ask that You continue to minister Your peace within my spirit. Father, I'm standing in faith and in agreement with the peace that You've gifted me. In Jesus' name, I pray, amen.

Peace

Day 22

Incline your Ear

"And let the peace of God rule in your hearts, to which also you were called in one body; and be thankful." – Colossians 3:15

☙

As you are going through life, look for the peace of God. Allow your spirit to be sensitive to the Lord's peace. The peace of the Holy Spirit is a good indicator that the Lord is pleased with your decision. When you're intentionally pursuing the peace of God over your life, your spirit becomes more sensitive to knowing and understanding God's will.

The goal is to pursue the Lord's peace. We are to allow His peace to govern us and direct our paths. As you are faithfully walking in Christ, you'll begin to receive a subtle peace in your soul. The more you incline your spirit and ear to the Lord as you wait for His peace, the more confident you'll become at knowing God's Word and will.

Dear Heavenly Father

Abba, in Jesus' name, I ask that You teach me to know Your voice. Father, I understand that knowing and learning Your voice is a process, and it takes trust and confidence in myself and faith in You. Father, I'm ready. I'm ready to learn Your voice and I'm ready to learn Your will. In Jesus' name, by faith, I receive Your peace that surpasses my understanding. Amen.

Day 23

Peace that Compels

"Pursue peace with all people, and holiness, without which no one will see the Lord" – Hebrews 12:14

୰

In this world, we are called to cohabit. We live amongst both saints and sinners – those who desire to pursue God, those who are on the fence, and those who outrightly refuse God. Regardless of where a person is spiritually, The Lord wants us to love and live in peace with all men.

It's easy for us to pursue peace with peaceable individuals. However, at times, it can be a bit hard for us to love and pursue peace with the unlovable. Nevertheless, when doing so, it not only strengthens you in the Lord, but it also draws others to Christ. Your God-given peace helps to knit the body of Christ in unity.

Dear Heavenly Father

Thank You, Lord, for showing me how to love and pursue peace with both peaceable and non-peaceable individuals. Father, it is an honor to be able to walk and share Your peace, so Lord, I thank You. In Jesus' name, I pray, amen.

Peace

Day 24

Effective in Wisdom

"Now, the fruit of righteousness is sown in peace by those who make peace." – James 3:18

☙

There's a scripture that says, *the effective, fervent prayer of a righteous man avails much* – this scripture is found in James 5:16. When it comes to sowing peace, it's correlated with praying and interceding for those in need. To effectively sow peace into good ground, you must also pursue inner peace. It'll be impossible to sow what you're lacking. You can only sow what you have.

I'm reminded of the story of the five 'wise' brides who had oil in their lampstand, yet their oil supply was not enough to share with others. When you're a peace carrier of the Lord, you not only fill up on peace for yourself, but for others. Whether you realize it or not, as you walk in peace, you become a magnet for those who need such God-given peace. The peace you carry will automatically compel others to walk in their God-given peace as well.

Dear Heavenly Father

Thank You for showing me that I can shift the atmosphere of doubt and strife into an environment of peace and peacemakers. Father, I ask that You help me to be mindful of Your Spirit, and to pursue Your peace at all costs. In Jesus' name, I pray, amen.

Day 25

Weapon of Warfare

"See that no one renders evil for evil to anyone, but always pursue what is good both for yourselves and for all." – 1 Thessalonians 5:15

☙

In this walk of life, you'll quickly learn that it's filled with all kinds of evil. You may be tempted to repay evil with evil, but don't. Employ peace. Peace is a silent but deadly weapon of war. Peace is one of the few fruits of the spirit that is also an Armor of God and a gift from Jesus. Walking in the Spirit of peace will avail you with a strategic weapon of warfare. Peace tears down hate, removes strife, and combats evil, all while leading others to Christ.

There's a saying that goes, 'you can attract more bees with honey.' The same is valid with the peace of God. Although it's not expressed in a manner in which we'll expect it, there is a never-ending hunger for peace. The world desires and needs the peace of God that you carry.

Dear Heavenly Father

Lord, I ask that You help me to strategically use the peace that You've given me for a weapon of warfare. Lord, help me to pursue peace in such a way that it will break barriers, defeat evil, and bring a breakthrough for Your glory. In Jesus' name, I pray, amen.

Peace

Day 26

Desires of the Heart

"Deceit is in the heart of those who devise evil, but counselors of peace have joy.' – Proverbs 12:20

☙

As a child of God, you have the privilege of being able to choose to walk in the path of good that is far from evil. The choices you make today will determine your outcome. Your preferences will either lead you far from God or closer to Him. Choose wisely.

Many have 'rejected' God. To be frank, God has rejected them. God tells us that He'll turn us over to a reprobate mind. He'll turn us over to the desires of our hearts and what we choose to pursue. Though others may intend to reject God after His many pursuits of tugging on their heart, God will finally turn them over to their desires. The Holy Spirit is just like you and me; He knows when He is not wanted nor desired. Consequently, God will reject evil and will reject man from His presence. Therefore, respond while you can. As God tugs on your heart, respond with 'Yes Lord.' Desire the Lord while His Spirit is still calling you.

Dear Heavenly Father

Lord, I ask that You give me a deeper longing for You. Father, increase my desire to know You and to become more intentional about pursuing the things of You. Lord, in Jesus' name, I pray, amen.

Day 27

Your Present Help

"Depart from evil and do good; Seek peace and pursue it." - Psalm 34:14

☙

Although we have freewill, The Lord is always cautioning us to pursue righteousness and live peaceable lives. On our own, this is impossible. However, our Helper, The Holy Spirit, was given as a gift so that we can navigate throughout life. The Holy Spirit is the one who cautions us when we stray off course. The Holy Spirit is the one who shows us the Father's heart and His will for our lives.

To pursue peace is to seek the Father's Spirit - His Holy Spirit.

Hey sis, as an encouragement, I want to let you know that you are doing a great job! God is so proud of you. If you haven't spoken over your life today, encourage yourself and remember that God sees you as the apple of His Eye. The Lord thinks that you are so precious even to the point that He saw fit to die for you so that you can live through Jesus. At this moment, the Lord desires to draw closer to you. He wants to build a more intimate relationship with you. As the Lord's daughter, He desires to shower you with His Holy Spirit so that you can navigate this thing called life and be filled with all the goodness of Jesus. Remain encouraged; God is for you!

Dear Heavenly Father

Lord, I thank You for showering me with Your Holy Spirit. Father, I ask that You bless me with more for Your gift and fruit of peace. Father, I desire to walk in Your will and pursue righteousness, but I need Your help. So, in Jesus' name, I thank You for sending Your Helper. Amen.

Peace

Day 28

The Preparation of the Gospel

"When a man's ways please the Lord, He makes even his enemies to be at peace with him." – Proverbs 16:7

☙

Peace is an excellent weapon of warfare. Ephesians 6:15 tells us to '*shod our feet with the preparation of the Gospel of Peace.*' The Word of God is sharper than every weapon and more powerful than any force. The moment you align yourself with the will of God, which is found in the Word of God, every opposition, every roadblock, every enemy, and every sickness must come under the authority and submission of Jesus Christ. Prepare yourself not with anger nor strife, but rather prepare yourself for battle with the Word of God, standing in His confidence and His authority.

The thing about coming into alignment with God is that everything else must submit and fall in place. All your enemies and opposition will be under the submission of Jesus. However, this is not to say that everything that you may consider 'bad' will vanish. No, this means that everything that had your back against the wall will come under the submission of Jesus Christ. If there is anything that is not the will of God, He will remove, correct it, and replace it, in Jesus' name.

Dear Heavenly Father

Lord God, I thank You for allowing me to be at peace, knowing that my enemies and opposition are under Your submission. Father, I know that in Jesus' name, I can rest assured because everything is in Your control. In Jesus' name, I pray, amen.

God's Strength

"The Lord will give strength to His people; The Lord will bless His people with peace. - Psalm 29:11

೦ಽ

The Strength of the Lord is your peace. There's a verse in the Bible that says, God's strength is made perfect in your weakness (2 Corinthians 12:9). The verse mentioned tells us that despite our apparent weakness, setbacks, and infirmities, God's strength is perfected in us. The Lord's strength is perfected not only because you have a lack, but also because you've submitted that lack to the Father.

There comes a time where you must show the Lord that you need His help. Too often do we parade around being 'everywoman', and only ending up frustrated and lacking the full peace of the Lord. We have caused ourselves to carry burdens that the Lord never intended for us to bear, or at least bear on our own. Your true peace and joy comes from a posture of being vulnerable and allowing the Father to grant you His peace, His strength, and His joy. But, you must let Him.

Dear Heavenly Father

Lord, I surrender. Father, no longer will I do life without You. Instead, Lord, I cast all my cares on You. Father, I welcome Your strength and Your peace. Lord, I know that Your supply is far better than mine. So, Father, I ask that You bless my feet and mind so that I can walk in Your peace. In Jesus' name, I pray, amen.

Peace

Day 30

Love with your Whole heart

"I will hear what God the Lord will speak, For He will speak peace To His people and to His saints; But let them not turn back to folly." - Psalm 85:8

☙

Many individuals sometimes have a relationship with the Father; they sometimes pray, and they sometimes seek Him. Often, this type of relationship is based on needing to get out of a pickle. The Lord knows that these 'sometime people' only go to Him for a 'sometime purpose.' However, have you ever asked yourself, *'why does the Lord still deliver them?'*

Despite their *sometimey* behavior, God is a hopeful Father. He longs for His children call on Him, go to Him, and stay with Him. Therefore, whenever the Father delivers you, His will is that you continue to walk with Him. Just like you and I, our Father, has feelings. It hurts God's heart when one of His children only go to Him for a 'sometime reason' yet, He still loves them.

Although we have the knowledge that the Lord answers His children's prayers and cries, let's not abuse that privilege. Just imagine being a parent to a child who only reaches out to you when it's convenient for them? You'll answer, but you'll feel hurt, and eventually get tired of that child or person. Choose today to wholeheartedly love the Lord and not only call on Him when you are in need.

Dear Heavenly Father

Lord, I ask that You give me a heart that is after Yours. Lord, forgive me for only seeking You when it's convenient for me. Father, I love You and desire to know more of You. In Jesus' name, I pray, amen.

Words for You

The peace of the world contains an illusion. One moment, you think you're walking in peace, only to find yourself trying to keep up with the latest trends, trying to please everyone or looking for the next best thing,

We spend countless hours trying to conform ourselves to the image and definition of this world that we neglect to rest at the Father's feet. The moment when you decide to rest will be when you understand the peace of God that surpasses all understanding. God's peace is understanding that you don't have to conform to the world to be renewed into the image of God. It's understanding that all that's required is to acknowledge Jesus.

As you honor and follow Jesus, you'll know that everything is in His control, and understand why Jesus said, "Peace I leave with you, My peace I give to you; not as the world gives, do I give to you. Let not your heart be troubled, neither let it be afraid." John 14:27 This surety is having confidence in God and allowing your mind and heart to be at ease with God's will.

Dear Heavenly Father

Lord, I pray that You show Your daughter how to rest in You. Father, I pray that she grows to love You more than before. Lord, I pray that she sees herself in Your eyes and understand that You want nothing but the best for Her. Lord, I ask that You renew her mind and transform her spirit in Jesus' name. Father, I trust that You're completing a good work in Her. In Jesus' name, I pray, amen.

Quiet Time

Prayer Request

Reflective Notes	**Reflective Questions**

Scriptures

Longsuffering

Day 31

Fruit over Gifting

"But the fruit of the Spirit is love, joy, peace, longsuffering, kindness, goodness, faithfulness." – Galatians 5:22

ଔ

There are nine fruits of the Spirit. All of which work together interchangeably to produce the will and evidence of God. God's fruit is what separates you from the world. The Fruit of the Spirit is your seal, given by God – this seal confirms that you're His child. Without this, you'll blend in with the world.

In addition to God granting us His fruit, He also imparts us with gifts for the purpose and edification of His work in ministry. However, gifts and callings are without repentance; they are irrevocable. Therefore, even an unbeliever can operate in the gifts that God gives. However, the Fruit of the Spirit being evident in your life will differentiate you as being a child of God working in His gifts.

As you take the time to develop your gifts and the fruit of the Spirit, be intentional about leaning into the fruit of longsuffering. Having the fruit of longsuffering will give you the capability to endure during hard times, and will ultimately keep you walking in the path that God has cleared for you.

Dear Heavenly Father

Lord, I ask that You keep my feet planted in You as You continue to increase me. Father, I understand that I must always have Your fruit working in me. So, Holy Spirit, I ask that You continue to prune me and mature me in Your image. In Your Son Jesus' name, I pray, amen.

Longsuffering

There's Produce in the Pruning

Day 32

"Or do you despise the riches of His goodness, forbearance, and longsuffering, not knowing that the goodness of God leads you to repentance?" – Romans 2:4

౭

It's hard to believe that the goodness of God involves a level of longsuffering. Longsuffering is evidence of God's goodness because the Lord uses the obstacles you've overcome to produce His fruit in you.

There will be countless trials, tribulations, setbacks, disappointments, heartbreaks, and moments where it seems as if God has forgotten you. During those moments, God is pruning and stretching you. The Lord stretches His children to produce sustainability and endurance.

In those moments when God is pruning you, you may want to give up and throw in the towel. Don't. Your endurance and ability to suffer long will be needed for where God is taking you. Your future requires the fruit of endurance be adequately cultivated. Without such, you may abandon parts of your purpose without even stepping a foot in the promised land. Your daily prayer should consist of asking the Lord to help you endure and finish your race to completion.

Dear Heavenly Father

Lord, I ask that You build Your fruit of longsuffering in me. Father, I desire to endure all that comes my way. Lord, I know that there are great rewards on the other side of my suffering. So Holy Spirit, help me to endure that which You require of me. In Jesus' name, I pray, amen.

Day 33

He is the Same

"For it was fitting for Him, for whom are all things and by whom are all things, in bringing many sons to glory, to make the captain of their salvation perfect through sufferings." – Hebrews 2:10

☙

Building an intimate relationship with our Sweet Savior is knowing that, other than His God nature, He is no different from you. The same way you suffer, Jesus suffered. The same way you're faced with making decisions, so was Jesus. The same way you experience joy, so does our Lord.

Our Savior, Jesus Christ, was placed on Earth to experience and also Exemplify His glory in all things. His purpose was to endure all that life can bring so that He can bring victory in our lives. Jesus endured so we can glory in Him.

Being clothed in the image of Christ is to be graced through the perfection of salvation that godly suffering brings. When you're in Christ, you may experience a level of suffering that you must endure. Although it may feel as if you're the only one suffering, know that you're not alone. You have the body of Christ interceding on your behalf. In addition to this, the Lord is your present help.

Dear Heavenly Father

Lord, I thank You for showing me that I am not alone. Thank You for gracing me with Your gift of love, joy, and longsuffering. Holy Spirit, I ask that You continue to help me and walk with me. Father, in Your Son Jesus' name, I pray, amen.

Longsuffering

Day 34

You're More than Enough

"And the Lord passed before him and proclaimed, the Lord, the Lord God, merciful and gracious, longsuffering, and abounding in goodness and truth." – Exodus 34:6

☙

In this section of Exodus, Moses had broken the first set of tablets that contain the original Ten Commandments. He'd broken the stones because, despite what the Lord said, the children of Israel were still sinning and worshipping foreign gods. Therefore, as their leader, Moses became fed up and was ready to throw in the towel.

Although Moses abandoned his assignment, God still saw him as more than enough. God required Moses to start his task again, and this time complete it. God was not worried about the objections of the people. The Lord's desire was for Moses to fulfill his purpose.

In life, you'll have obstacles and objections. However, your faith must be rooted in God so that you can endure all forms of roadblocks. The Lord's will is that you'll rise above your hindrances and remain faithful in walking in your God-ordained purpose, by not growing weary due to your current situation.

Dear Heavenly Father

Lord, I ask that You send Your Holy Spirit to help me to remain faithful when my back is against the wall. Lord, I need Your help, I cannot do life without You. In Jesus' name, I pray, amen.

Day 35

The Power of your Resistance

"Therefore, submit to God. Resist the devil and he will flee from you."
– James 4:7

ೲ
Sin and destruction are inevitable. However, you are not bound by this. God has given you a way to escape. As you submit your life to God, the Holy Spirit will show you how to resist the Devil. It's not an easy task. Resisting the Devil is a mission that will take lots of faith, patience, and endurance. As a child of God, you'll need to build your faith muscle and depend on Him. The Lord is your way out of trouble. In Him are the fullness, riches, and ways of life. Seek the Lord in all situations, and He'll provide your every need.

Resisting the devil is possible, but you must seek the Lord. Although we are built on knowing good and evil, we're not strong enough to sustain our own good works. We need the Lord's help in all situations. One of the keys to obtaining God's help is humbling yourself and removing pride from your heart. For pride says, 'Lord, I got this,' but humility says, 'Lord, I need Your help. Help me.'

Dear Heavenly Father
Lord, I am not too proud to ask for Your help. Father, I need Your help, sin is inevitable, and I choose to walk in Your path. Father, I need You to help me resist the Devil. Lord, I know in Your name Satan must flee. In Jesus' name, I pray, amen.

Longsuffering

Day 36

As you Wait

"The Lord is not slack concerning His promise, as some count slackness, but is longsuffering toward us, not willing that any should perish but that all should come to repentance." – 2 Peter 3:9

ଓଃ

So, you've been waiting for the promises of the Lord to be fulfilled in your life. It seems as if they'll never come to fruition. It almost feels as if everyone is passing you and that God has forgotten you. He hasn't. God is many things; however, one thing God is not, is forgetful about His promises. Although it appears as if your desires will never come to pass, trust that God is a faithful God. The Lord will see to it that His purpose is fulfilled concerning you.

I know you've been waiting; However, I want to encourage you to keep waiting. As you wait, choose to wait gracefully. This means that your hope and faith are anchored in the Lord. You trust in God knowing that every closed door is a door that the Father intended to close. In addition, every open door is a door that only the Lord can open. As you wait gracefully, continue to refuel on the Word of God and meditate on His will concerning your life.

Dear Heavenly Father

Lord, I ask that You help me to wait on You. Father, show me the grace and power of waiting in Your will. Holy Spirit, I ask that You help me to stay in alignment with God and not walk or move in front of Him. In Jesus' name, I pray, amen.

Day 37
Having done all... Stand

"Therefore, as the elect of God, holy and beloved, put on tender mercies, kindness, humility, meekness, longsuffering" – Colossians 3:12

☙

Though it is not explicitly stated, longsuffering is an armor of God. In addition to Colossians 3:12, which tells us to put *'on'* longsuffering, Ephesians 6:13 tells us to stand after we've put on the will of God, which is His armor. Standing in righteousness is an act of defense against the kingdom of darkness. You have a war cry in your endurance and in your longsuffering. Your war cry says, *although I'm hard-pressed, I will not be shaken. No matter how my odds look, I will keep my trust in the Lord.*

The fruit of longsuffering that the Lord wants to prune out of you contains victory. The moment you posture yourself with the Lord and wait on His will and timing, anxiety, fear, and doubt will subside. I'm not promising that it'll completely go away, but standing in the Lord will make enduring through such times easier.

Dear Heavenly Father

Lord, I ask that You allow my feet to be planted in You. Father, as I seek You, strengthen my fruit of longsuffering so that I may stand. Lord, I trust You and Father I thank You! In Your Son Jesus' name, I pray, amen.

Longsuffering

Day 38

Whose Desires are you Pursuing

"And we know that all things work together for good to those who love God, to those who are the called according to His purpose." - Romans 8:28

೫

Romans 8:28 work in three folds. All things will work together for good. However, loving God is not the only key. In addition to love, you must ask yourself; *'am I in alignment with God?' 'am I working according to God's will, or am I working out of my own desires?'*

Due to the mere fact that we are humans living in a sin-filled world, we will experience tests and trials. However, the desires that you pursue will dictate your outcome. If you're walking according to your flesh and of this world, then there is no promise that anything will work out for your good. However, if you're a child of God, then everything will work out in your favor, since you not only love the Lord, but are also walking in His will.

At this moment, you may be figuring out how to walk according to God's purpose, and that's okay. The best way to figure out someone's desires is to get to know them. Just like in a relationship, you'll know God by spending time with Him. This means that you're reading your Bible, going to church, getting connected with other believers, etc. I want to encourage you to spend intentional time with God as you get to know Him and His purpose for you.

Dear Heavenly Father
Lord, teach me to hear Your voice so that I can know You and always walk in Your will. In Jesus' name, I pray, amen.

Day 39
Allow Patience to have its Perfect Work

"You also be patient. Establish your hearts, for the coming of the Lord is at hand. Do not grumble against one another, brethren, lest you be condemned. Behold, the Judge is standing at the door!" – James 5:8-9

☙

Let's be honest, it's not easy walking in longsuffering. Longsuffering requires you to endure tough times, and it might mean that you'll be dealt the brunt end of things. However, walking in the will of God means that we need longsuffering to be developed in us. As you grow and develop in such fruit, by default, you'll also strengthen the gift of patience and peace. Longsuffering is not a fruit that can be developed on its own. You'll need the help and presence of other fruit and gifts. Your sustainability and endurance depend on the fullness of Jesus.

As you know by now, I want to encourage you. As you're being developed and strengthened in longsuffering, keep your hope. You'll have trying times, but remember as you wait on the Lord, He will renew your strength. The Lord will meet you and endow you with everything that it takes to nurture His seed and bring you to His place of destiny.

Dear Heavenly Father

Lord, I thank You for giving me Your seed of longsuffering. Father, I ask that You continue to guide me every step of the way. In Jesus' name, I thank You and pray, amen.

Longsuffering

Day 40

For all things, There is a season

"I know how to be abased, and I know how to abound. Everywhere and in all things I have learned both to be full and to be hungry, both to abound and to suffer need." - Philippians 4:12

☙

There is a season for everything. There is a season to endure, and there is a season to rest. In all seasons, choose to acknowledge God in all your ways. Choose to know and understand that as a child of God who loves the Lord and is walking in His will, everything will work out in your favor.

As you grow to understand the seasons that God places you in, you will soon realize that every season of your life has a set timing. With an exception to God's Word, nothing on earth last forever. Therefore, instead of walking in sorrow, choose to see the joy and good. There is always a silver lining at the end. So, why not rejoice in all things and embrace the process to your purpose.

Dear Heavenly Father

Lord, help me to see that Your hand is always over my life working for my good. Help me to acknowledge that You will never leave me nor forsake me. Father, help me to understand that weeping only lasts for a night, but Your Joy will always meet me even in the midst of my sorrows. Father, I thank You for strengthening me and grooming me in Your favor. In Your Son Jesus' name, I pray, amen.

Words for You

In life, there will be setbacks and disappointments. How you embrace them will determine how each situation will be used in your life. It's best to look at as much – if not, all situations as a learning tool, and as an anchor in God's will and favor over your life.

Jeremiah 1:5 says that before you were born, God knew you. God knows of every situation, both good and bad, that has and will happen in your life. Neither you nor your situation surprises God. Therefore, work towards embracing all that God has for you and know that as a child of God who is walking in the Will of the Lord, everything will work out in your favor.

Use this moment to grow in the fruit of longsuffering and endure what the Lord places in your hand. Now, there is a difference between needing to build endurance from a God-led situation and a situation that causes you to suffer due to your own mistakes, desires, or disobedience. For this reason, it is vital that you're not leaning on your own understanding, but you're acknowledging the Lord in all your ways. Acknowledging God will ensure that He is leading and guiding you along your path.

Dear Heavenly Father

Lord, I ask that You help Your daughter to depend and lean on You. Father guide her footsteps as she walks along Your path. Lord, I thank You for showing her Your grace. Lord, she loves You and desires to know more of You. Father, I ask that You endow her with Your presence. In Your Son Jesus' name, I pray, amen.

Quiet Time

Prayer Request

Reflective Notes | **Reflective Questions**

Scriptures

Kindness

My Sweet Savior • 90 Day Devotional

Day 41

No Respecter of Person

"What is desired in a man is kindness, and a poor man is better than a liar." – Proverbs 19:22

☙

To be spirit-led is to show kindness and to walk in love. This means to show the same level of grace and favor to the least as you would the greatest. God favors and admires a kind soul, for it's a wealthy asset of God. It's better to treat a man in a Christ-like manner, than to walk around with pride and a prudent heart.

SIDE NOTE: You don't have to like someone to show kindness. Kindness is a God-given, universal trait that is accessible to all. Being able to walk in godly maturity and show the same measure of grace and kindness to your enemies as you do your friends is a gift and privilege. However, knowing how to show grace and walking in kindness does require discernment and strength. Therefore, allow God to lead you and guide you in wisdom.

Dear Heavenly Father

Lord, I ask that You show me how to walk in kindness with Your godly wisdom. Show me how to show the same measure to grace to all men. Father, I ask that You strengthen my discernment so that I know how to show kindness while walking in Your integrity and in Your armor. In Jesus' name, I pray, amen.

Kindness

Day 42

It takes Unconditional Love to produce Kindness

"And now may the Lord show kindness and truth to you. I also will repay you this kindness, because you have done this thing." - 2 Samuel 2:6

☙

As you walk in kindness, it may appear as if your good works are going unnoticed. Perhaps, you may even feel as if you are being pushed over and neglected. If so, I want to assure you that we have a Just God who sits high and looks low. Your Father in Heaven sees your heart and your passion to pursue kindness and justice for all men. The Lord knows your desires. As a result, He's sending people who will help lead you to your purpose and bless you abundantly.

Today, practice walking in unconditional love. Choose to love and show kindness to all, even those who persecute you. In addition, ask the Lord to give you discernment and guidance as you walk in His spirit. As a child of God who walks with God's heart, it takes wisdom and understanding to know the difference between placing yourself in compromising situations where you can be taken advantage of, and walking in the Lord's authority as you share the love of Christ.

Dear Heavenly Father

Father, I desire to be a light within this world. So, Lord, I thank You for gracing me with this heart's desire as I pursue Your godly justice. Father, I ask that You continue to guide and lead me. In Your Son, Jesus' name Lord I pray, amen.

Day 43

You are Not Forgotten

"For His merciful kindness is great toward us, And the truth of the Lord endures forever. Praise the Lord!" - Psalm 117:2

☙

As a Father, the Lord wants nothing but the best for you. It's important to know that you are a precious gem to the Father. You are the apple of His eye. He cares so much for you that He sent His only Son to pay the price of death so that you can be reconciled back to Him. The Lord God wants you to draw near to Him as He restores and molds you back into His image, which He has spoken over you.

There will be moments where it seems as if God has forgotten about you, and you may even feel abandoned. However, during your toughest hours, remember God's truth. Remember the thoughts that the Lord thinks towards you. The truth of God will reassure you that you're neither forsaken, nor are you forgotten.

Some great tips to remembering God's Word are to meditate on His Scripture and to journal your prayers, concerns and the revelation you've received from your reading and quiet time.

Dear Heavenly Father

Lord, I thank You for bringing all things to remembrance. Father, I ask that You show me how to walk in Your boldness with confidence. In Jesus' name, I pray, amen.

Kindness

Day 44

His Loving Kindness

"But when the kindness and the love of God our Savior toward man appeared, not by works of righteousness which we have done, but according to His mercy He saved us, through the washing of regeneration and renewing of the Holy Spirit." – Titus 3:4-5

☙

There is nothing more that we can do that will provoke the Love of God towards us. The Lord loves us simply because we're His. Yes, there are times when God may be disappointed and disapprove of our actions, but it does not eliminate His love.

The Love of the Lord is a cleansing type of love. His love causes all men who accept to become renewed and made whole in His presence.

Choose today to see that just like natural parents, the Lord at times will rebuke and chastise you – lovingly. He does so to purify you into a renewed spirit in Him.

Dear Heavenly Father

Lord, I desire to become whole before You. So, Father, I ask that You continue to cleanse my soul and renew my mind. Father, I thank You for choosing me as Your child. In Jesus' name, I pray, amen.

Day 45

Renewed in His Presence

"And raised us up together, and made us sit together in the heavenly places in Christ Jesus, that in the ages to come He might show the exceeding riches of His grace in His kindness toward us in Christ Jesus." – Ephesians 2:6-7

☙

If you remember one thing today, remember that Jesus loves you dearly. The Lord's intentions are for you to experience His love, become transformed in His presence, and share His love and mercy towards others.

As you continue to grow in Christ, you'll begin to understand that in every situation, God's hand is resting over your life. The Lord uses His Holy Spirit to give you nudges and guidance in the direction you're to walk in. Therefore, it's important that you seek the Holy Spirit and wait on His presence and assurance. As the Lord leads you, He's leading you into wealth by placing you in a posture of holiness and purity.

Dear Heavenly Father

Lord, I ask that You enrich my soul with Your goodness and mercy. Father, I know that the things of this world are to pass away. However, You, oh Lord, are The Everlasting God, so I wish to be conformed in Your image. In Your Son Jesus' name, I pray, amen.

Love that Compels

Day 46

"Love suffers long and is kind; love does not envy; love does not parade itself, is not puffed up." – 1 Corinthians 13:4

☙

Pure and genuine love is humility, it's caring, and it's not self-seeking. Love is having a pure heart and godly motives, while walking in care and compassion. Love is being able to share God's heart for His people, all while loving on yourself.

The key facet of love is simply loving others as you would have them to love you. Or in biblical terms, "Just as you want men to do to you, you also do to them." – Luke 6:31

God is a Gentleman and is patient towards you. The Lord is faithful to show kindness towards you simply because He loves you. Likewise, just as you're made in the image of God, you too, have the Lord's strength to show pure kindness to others simply because the love of God compels you.

Dear Heavenly Father

Lord, I thank You for sending Your Holy Spirit to show me how to love and show kindness to others. Father, I desire to walk in Your pure love and show grace as I receive not only grace from you but grace from others. In Your Son, Jesus' name, I do pray, amen.

Day 47

The Same Grace

"And be kind to one another, tenderhearted, forgiving one another, even as God in Christ forgave you." – Ephesians 4:32

ଔ

When asked, Jesus said one should forgive someone seventy times seven times. Not that we should take account of how many times we should forgive someone, but rather, forgive without measure. Forgive those who've hurt you, persecuted you, and even sinned against you. Although forgiving someone may prove to be challenging, we forgive not only for the sake of that individual, but also for our sake.

As a child being called into the likeness of Jesus, it's our natural response to forgive, show grace and kindness to those who've hurt us. The reason being that in, Jeremiah 31:34, God said, "For I will forgive their iniquity, and their sin I will remember no more." Being created in the image of God, having a heart of forgiveness, is engraved in our DNA. However, due to living in a world that is filled with hurt and pain, it's hard to genuinely walk in the spirit of forgiveness.

Therefore, as an encouragement, strive to forgive and show the same type of love and grace towards everyone. If someone does not receive you, do as Jesus did in Matthew 10:14 and walk with a clear conscience knowing that you've done your part and loved as Jesus would.

Dear Heavenly Father

Lord, I ask that You show me how to walk in the spirit of grace and compassion. Holy Spirit, I desire to show forgiveness to all men; therefore, teach me how to forgive as Jesus would. In Jesus' name, I pray, amen.

Kindness

Day 48

To Walk in His Ways

"Blessed be the Lord, For He has shown me His marvelous kindness in a strong city!" – Psalm 31:21

☙

Despite the innumerable times we've sinned against God as a people and nation; God is still kind. The Lord chooses to show His grace of kindness towards His people. It's nothing that we've done or could do that will incite the love of Christ. Jesus loves us because we're born in His image and created by His hands.

Many use the grace of God as a freewill pass to conform to the ways of the world. However, this is not an excuse to continue to walk in a sin-filled behavior. The Lord's grace should compel you to live wholly before Him.

Although God is merciful, choose today to not take His love for granted. Decide that from this day forward, every day of your life will be lived as one that is pleasing to our Sweet Savior. As an encouragement, your walk does not have to look like everyone else's, for the Father uniquely created you. Walk in the ways of which God has called you.

Dear Heavenly Father

Lord, I ask that You continue to clear my path so that I may walk in the ways that You're leading me. Father, I desire to do Your will. So, Father, I ask that You resound Your voice so that I may be guided by You. Holy Spirit, as my Helper, I ask that You help me to live a life that is pleasing to the Father. In Jesus' name, I pray, amen.

Day 49

Freedom in Christ

"So rend your heart, and not your garments; Return to the Lord your God, for He is gracious and merciful, slow to anger, and of great kindness; And He relents from doing harm." – Joel 2:13

ଓ

You were once dead in your trespasses, due to sin. However, as a result of you committing your life to Christ, you now have access to life eternally. The moment you decided to say yes to Jesus, God relented from giving you your just reward, which would have resulted in death.

God is a just Father, and all He wants is for His children to love, honor, and accept Him. His desires are for His children to walk in the fullness of His holiness and love.

Despite your circumstances and your past, choose to love God wholeheartedly. Choose to surrender your heart to the Lord. God is a loving Father. Because you are His child, He chooses not to remember your sins of yesterday. He has forgiven you of all that you've ever done; the Lord has even healed you from your past hurt and shame. Therefore, you are free to love, free to worship and free to live in Christ Jesus. Give Him your heart, give Him your hand, He's waiting for you.

Dear Heavenly Father

Lord, I ask that You help me to surrender the hidden things that I've kept from You. Father, help me to live a life that is completely surrendered and dependent on You. Holy Spirit, I thank You for being my Helper, in Jesus' name, I pray, amen.

Kindness

Day 50

Fruit of Life

"To godliness brotherly kindness, and to brotherly kindness love." – 2 Peter 1:7

☙

2 Peter 1:5-11 is such a powerful scripture as it outlines the way of a fruitful life. It read;

> [5] But also for this very reason, giving all diligence, add to your faith virtue, to virtue knowledge, [6] to knowledge self-control, to self-control perseverance, to perseverance godliness, [7] to godliness brotherly kindness, *and to brotherly kindness love.* [8] For if these things are yours and abound, *you* will be neither barren nor unfruitful in the knowledge of our Lord Jesus Christ. [9] For he who lacks these things is shortsighted, even to blindness, and has forgotten that he was cleansed from his old sins. [10] Therefore, brethren, be even more diligent to make your call and election sure, for if you do these things you will never stumble; [11] for so an entrance will be supplied to you abundantly into the everlasting kingdom of our Lord and Savior Jesus Christ.

The stipulations of these scriptures are clear; as you have faith, walk in the spirit of godly ethics with excellence. As you continue to increase in faith, knowledge, wisdom and understanding of the calling and purposes God has set before you, pursue love and kindness. Love is the main ingredient. For love is the driving force of living in Christ and living amongst others while sharing the love of Christ.

Dear Heavenly Father

Lord, I thank You for showing me how to walk in love. Father, I ask that You bring me into a deeper level and understanding of what love is and what love means to You. In Jesus' name, I pray, amen.

Words for You

As you sit at the feet of Jesus, allow Him to pour His oil over you. His oil is His anointing. His oil is His way and will for your life. In the Lord's oil flows rivers of kindness and everlasting life. Romans 8:1 tells us that "there *is* no condemnation to those who are in Christ Jesus, who do not walk according to the flesh, but according to the Spirit." This means that as you spend time with Jesus, the oil of kindness that He pours over you will remove your past shame and sins. In exchange, the Lord will give you a new name and a new identity. The only thing that the Father requires is your heart.

As you give the Lord your 'yes,' He will then begin to transform your mind and give you an abundance of love and kindness. In love and in kindness is the fulfillment of all things that Jesus requires. Kindness is the evidence of love, and without love, there's nothing.

As we close out this section on Kindness, I want to encourage you to pursue love. If need be, turn back to our first chapter and allow that segment of your devotional to resonate with your spirit. For in love is the strength to walk out in the fullness of Jesus with full authority and kindness.

Dear Heavenly Father

Lord, I thank You for allowing Your daughter to pursue Your kindness with love, grace and peace. Father, I ask that You send Your Holy Spirit to help her walk with boldness as she shares Your love and be an example to others. In Jesus' name, I pray, amen.

Quiet Time

Prayer Request

Reflective Notes | **Reflective Questions**

Scriptures

Goodness

Day 51

In the Pursuit of...

"Let love be without hypocrisy. Abhor what is evil. Cling to what is good." – Romans 12:9

☙

As a child of God who seeks the Lord, His pure love will permeate through you. The gift of love and goodness that God allows to flow from you to others is a precious gift that should be nurtured and handled with great joy.

There's a scripture that can be found in Luke 12:48 that states, "*For everyone to whom much is given, from him much will be required; and to whom much has been committed, of him they will ask the more.*" When Jesus gifted you His gift of pure love, joy, kindness and goodness, He expected you to use it for His good and glory. Using God's gift for good requires that you set yourself apart in such a way that you are a beacon of light to the world.

As a light, who is also an ambassador of Jesus, you're drawing souls closer to Him. Therefore, handling your light with care and compassion is crucial. Regardless of where you are in your walk of faith, how you treat others behind closed doors as well as yourself is the first thing that gets noticed. So be mindful and intentional to show genuine love and goodness.

Dear Heavenly Father

In Jesus' name, Father, I thank You for giving me Your gift of love, joy, kindness and goodness. Father, I ask that Your Holy Spirit continue to guide me to keep my feet in the pursuit of good. In Your Son Jesus' name, I pray, amen.

Day 52

By the Blood of the Lamb

"Do not be overcome by evil, but overcome evil with good." - Romans 12:21

☙

Every believer of Jesus Christ has the power and ability to overcome evil. The power to overcome evil is a specific gift that the Lord Jesus Christ has gifted us. This gift was given the moment He conquered hell and death for all who believe in Him.

Galatians 3:27 tells us that because we've been baptized into Christ, we also have the garment of Christ. To have the garment of Christ means to have the same capabilities that Christ has. The capabilities of Jesus are limitless, and they include; walking in love, healing, righteousness, and overcoming evil.

I think it's also important to note that having the garment of Christ does not exempt us from obstacles caused by tribulation and the everyday norms of life. As a matter of fact, since we have put on Christ, we should understand that just as Christ experienced tribulations and overcame evil, so can we. *For we overcome by the Blood of the Lamb and the word of our testimony.* – Revelation 12:11

Dear Heavenly Father

Lord God, I thank You for giving me Your strength to overcome evil and the tribulations of this world. Father, I know that it's only by the Blood of Jesus in which I can overcome and rise with Christ. So, Father, In Jesus' name, I thank You, amen.

Day 53

Greater is One Day

"The Lord is righteous in all His ways, Gracious in all His works." - Psalm 145:17

☙

You may not fully understand what God is doing in your life, but will you trust Him? Will you trust the Lord knowing that He will never leave you nor forsake you? Will you trust Jesus knowing that He has given you His Spirit to guide, deliver, and redeem you? Will you trust the Father knowing that He is a good, good Father?

The Lord is waiting for your answer. It does not have to be a 'yes' at this moment, but the Lord desires your 'yes.'

Having the understanding that God is a just God and a rewarder of those who diligently seek Him should grant us a heart posture of one that is totally dependent and surrendered. This will require vulnerability, and I'd be the first to say that being vulnerable is not easy. Therefore, you may not be in a hurry to say 'yes,' and that's okay. I want to encourage you to give God, daily yeses, take it one day at a time and allow Him to complete His perfect work in you.

As you go day by day, your one-day yes will turn into a lifetime of yeses.

Dear Heavenly Father

Lord God, I understand that this walk with You is neither a marathon nor a sprint. So, Father, I ask that day by day, You transform my life. Lord, I also ask that with every passing day, You grant me a greater desire for Your love and will. In Your Son Jesus' name, I pray, amen.

Goodness

Day 54

For His Glory

"The Lord is good, A stronghold in the day of trouble; And He knows those who trust in Him." – Nahum 1:7

☙

Too often do we hear, *'if God is real and if God is a good Father, then why does He allow bad things to happen?' 'Why are bad and unfortunate things happening to me and to those around me?' 'The Lord is supposed to save us and only cause good to happen since He is, a good Father.'*

The answer to these questions can be found in numerous verses, all ranging from us having free will to, whatever a man sows, he will reap. However, today, we're going to focus on John 9:3, which states: "Neither this man nor his parents sinned, but that the works of God should be revealed in him."

It's important to note and understand that God is a Good Father. He knows all that you're going through and all that you've been through. As a child of God, the Lord desires to use every circumstance for the manifestation of your good. Simply trust and believe that the Lord wishes to use your life to glorify Himself; therefore, all things will work out for your good, because you love Him.

Dear Heavenly Father

In Jesus' name, I ask that You help me to see Your goodness in every situation. Help me to know that You are a good and loving Father, and Your desires are that I prosper and flourish in You. In Jesus' name, I pray, amen.

Day 55

In His Goodness and Mercy

"And God *is* able to make all grace abound toward you, that you, always having all sufficiency in all *things,* may have an abundance for every good work." – 2 Corinthians 9:8

☙

Romans 8:28, along with 2 Corinthians 9:8 are perfect scriptures to meditate on. With all things, it's important to know that as a child of God who loves Him and desires to fulfill His will, God will make His grace abound towards you.

God's grace means that all things will work out for your good. God's grace means that no matter what your circumstances are, the goodness of the Lord will prevail. As a reminder, remember to look towards the hill, for that's where your help comes from *(see Psalms 121:1).* Your help, your grace, your breakthrough comes from the goodness and mercy of Christ Jesus. There is a Light on the other side of the tunnel. You will not only acknowledge that Light, but you will also experience that Light. Hold on to the faith that God has gifted you with and push forward with all perseverance.

Dear Heavenly Father

Lord God, I thank You for establishing me in Your goodness. Lord, I ask that You guide my every step so that I may walk in Your will with boldness and confidence. Father, help me to acknowledge that there are rays of sunshine and hope that's in my future. Help me to know and understand that You desire to endow me with Your goodness and Your mercy. In Your Son Jesus' name, I pray, amen.

Goodness

Day 56

In Jesus' Name

"Trust in the Lord, and do good; Dwell in the land, and feed on His faithfulness." Psalm 37:3

಄

This scripture is like healing for the soul. All throughout the Bible, the Lord instructs us to dwell with Him, honor Him, trust Him, and Love Him. Psalms 37:3 is the epitome of God's desire for His children. The moment you get a hold of this scripture and understand its healing properties, that moment, you will be set free. For God is a good Father, and His desires are to see His children whole and set free in Him.

This world has a way of creating a host of bondage among the children of God. No matter what's binding you, there's freedom and deliverance in Jesus' name. Your healing, freedom and deliverance comes the moment you trust in the Lord, do His will, dwell in His presence, and eat the Bread of Life, which is His Word and way.

Dear Heavenly Father

Lord thank You for showing me Your goodness, thank You for showing me that my healing and deliverance comes the moment I honor You and dwell in Your presence. Holy Spirit, I ask that You help me to remain steadfast in You and to honor You with my life. In your Son Jesus' name, I pray, amen.

Day 57

Ambassadors of Excellence

"But also for this very reason, giving all diligence, add to your faith virtue, to virtue knowledge, to knowledge self-control, to self-control perseverance, to perseverance godliness, to godliness brotherly kindness, and to brotherly kindness love." – 2 Peter 1:5-7

ର

As the Body of Christ, we're comprised of many members, not just ourselves. We must look beyond ourselves and consider the Body as a Whole. It's God's will that every member that's a part of the Body of Christ functions as a knit unit with love and harmony. Ephesians 4:13 tells us this very truth. As the body of Christ, in addition to being members of one another, we're also Christ's ambassadors.

As an ambassador of Christ, you're called to a higher standard. We were created to be set apart from the world. We were created to be that example and the light that the world so desperately needs. As an Ambassador, we are Christ representation; therefore, we're called to uphold His integrity amongst ourselves and within the world.

Dear Heavenly Father

Lord, I ask that You show me how to be Your excellent ambassador. Father, help me to mirror the ways You've set before me. Lord, I thank You for choosing to set me apart and consider me as an heir and partaker of Your Kingdom. In Jesus' name, I pray, amen.

Goodness

Day 58

Declare and Decree

"Who gave Himself for us, that He might redeem us from every lawless deed and purify for Himself His own special people, zealous for good works." – Titus 2:14

෩
When Christ died, He died for you. Christ died so that you may have life and life more abundantly. The Lord died so that you may live in freedom. Jesus died so that you're no longer a subject of sin, but an overcomer through Him. In all things, remember this truth. Keep this at the forefront of everything you do. In Christ Jesus, you have liberty.

It's time to start speaking life over yourself. No longer will you sit in self-pity, bruising your spirit. Take the time and declare God's Word over your life.

You are an overcomer. – Romans 8:27
You are the head and NOT the tail. – Deuteronomy 28:13
You are above and not beneath. – Deuteronomy 28:13
You are the apple of God's Eye. – Psalm 17:8
You are the Lord's beloved. – Songs of Solomon 6:3
You are fearfully and wonderfully made. – Psalm 139:14
You are God's masterpiece. – Ephesians 2:10
You are the daughter of the Highest God. – Psalm 82:6
You are an ambassador of Jesus Christ. – 2 Corinthians 5:20

Dear Heavenly Father

Father, if I ever forget who I am and What Your mercy has done for me, remind me. Minister Your Words over my soul. Lord, continue to speak life in me. Father, I know You no longer remember my sins and faults, so Lord, help me to see myself the way You see me. In Jesus' name, I pray, amen.

Day 59

Where One Go, The Other will Follow

"Do not be deceived: 'Evil company corrupts good habits." - 1 Corinthians 15:33

૪

There's a saying that tells us not to be *unequally yoked*. The reason being is that when cattle are yoked together, where one goes, the other will automatically follow. Therefore, as a child of God, if you're yoked or even among bad company, your chances of going down the same path as they are much greater than the chances of them being swayed into the righteous path. Therefore, you must be mindful of the company you keep and the influence you allow around you.

When most believers come into the fold of Jesus Christ, they often feel as if they should drop every person that is not a believer as well as those who are not walking down a path that is like theirs. However, being mindful of the company you keep is more like using discernment and allowing the Holy Spirit to guide you – this may not mean dropping an individual completely. Instead, be mindful of how you're being influenced by taking a stand not to be yoked and swayed into the things of this world. This will require you to hold fast to your beliefs and choose to honor the Lord, with your body, soul and Spirit.

Dear Heavenly Father

Lord, I ask that You grant me an outpour of Your discernment. Father, show me how to keep Your good company. Lord show me how to be in the world but not of the world. Lord, show me how to hear from You as You guide and lead me. In Jesus' name, I pray, amen.

Goodness

Day 60

Amongst the Greatest

"Then you will understand righteousness and justice, equity and every good path." – Proverbs 2:9

☙

Jesus said that if you ask anything in His name, then it will be given to you. Therefore, if you ask for discernment, wisdom and understanding from the Lord, then you will receive that. The Lord wants to shower you with His gifts and knowledge. Therefore, you will have great gain when you receive it.

Above all else, having wisdom, discernment and understanding in the Lord are one of the greatest gifts you can ever receive. With such, you will understand the ways and the will of the Father. You will receive great gain. Your path in the Lord will be made straight, and you will be perfected in Him. Receiving wisdom, discernment and understanding is all a matter of asking the God for it, believing by faith that He has given it and trusting in Him to use it. As you increase in faith, the stronger each gift will become. Each gift becomes stronger as a result of an increase in your intimacy, relationship, and faith in the Lord.

Dear Heavenly Father

Lord, I thank You for showing me that Your goodness and gifts are freely given. Father help me to increase in faith so that I can walk in Your wisdom, discernment and understanding. Father, I desire to know Your will and Your ways. So, Father, help me. In Jesus' name, I pray, amen.

Words for You

One of the greatest aspects of the Lord is His goodness. The Lord is faithful in showing Goodness to all His children. Yes, there are times where it appears as if God is not merciful, and as if your world is falling apart. However, it's important to remember that God is a good Father, and ALL things will work out for your good because you love the Lord, and you are called according to His purpose – Romans 8:28.

It's also important to note that though there are 'bad' things in the world, and bad things may happen to you and your loved ones, know that God is not physically harming you, nor is it His desire to do so. God wants nothing but the best for you, and He wants to see you flourish in Him. However, as a result of unfortunate circumstances that may arise, as a child of God, He will see to it that you overcome it all. In addition to being an overcomer, you will become wiser through your experiences, and then you will understand the meaning of Romans 8:28.

Dear Heavenly Father

Lord, I pray that You govern my sister. Father help her to see that in all things, You are a good Father. Lord, help her to acknowledge You in all her ways. Father, I pray that she grows in the wisdom, discernment, and understanding of Your love, will, and way. In Jesus' name, I pray, amen.

Quiet Time

Prayer Request

Reflective Notes | **Reflective Questions**

Scriptures

Faithfulness

Day 61

But will you remain faithful?

"Therefore, you shall be careful to do as the Lord your God has commanded you; you shall not turn aside to the right hand or to the left. You shall walk in all the ways which the Lord your God has commanded you, that you may live and that it may be well with you, and that you may prolong your days in the land which you shall possess." – Deuteronomy 5:32-33 32

୰

You may not fully understand all that God is doing in this season, but please remain faithful. Remain faithful, because there's a breakthrough on the other side of your obedience. Your future, the futures of your children, and the futures of children's children are depending on your obedience and your ability to remain steadfast in the Lord.

We've all heard of generational curses! Generational curses are curses or continued habits and situations that continue down your bloodline. Now, what if I told you that there are more generational victories that are attached to you than there are generational curses; will you contend for them?

As a result of Jesus conquering death and delivering life and victory to all who believe in Him, your generational victories are found in your obedience in Jesus Christ. The Lord said that if we take up our cross and follow Him daily, then we would obtain life (*see Luke 9:23*). Therefore, we should make a conscious choice of following Jesus daily.

Dear Heavenly Father

In Jesus' name, Lord, I ask that You help me to contend for my faith as I pursue You daily. Lord, in Jesus' name, I trust You, amen.

Faithfulness

Day 62

You are Treasured in Heaven

"Now therefore, if you will indeed obey My voice and keep My covenant, then you shall be a special treasure to Me above all people; for all the earth is Mine." – Exodus 19:5

☙

The Lord is not slack concerning the fulfillment of His promises to you. As you continue in your faith and in your fellowship with Jesus, you will be rewarded with heavenly riches.

Many of us look towards the world for validation and rewards for our efforts, while supplies last, you may receive your validation – but this is temporal. However, as followers and believers of Jesus Christ who earnestly seek the Father, while the Lord may reward us publicly, we have eternal riches stored up in Heaven. Heavenly riches far outweigh anything that this earth can provide.

I want to take a moment and encourage you to remain steadfast in the Lord. Although trusting in the Lord can prove to be challenging at times, your obedience and faithfulness are treasured in Heaven. Keep striving to remain faithful and loving in Jesus' name.

Dear Heavenly Father

Lord, I thank You for planting my feet and steading my mind in You. Lord, in Jesus' name, I will serve and honor You all the days of my life. Father, I love and adore You. In Your Son Jesus' name, I pray, amen.

Day 63

Great Gains

"Therefore, let those who suffer according to the will of God commit their souls to Him in doing good, as to a faithful Creator." - 1 Peter 4:19

☙

Romans 8:18 tells us "that the sufferings of this present time are not worthy *to be compared* with the glory which shall be revealed in us." As children of God, our promise of life is only found in committing our ways to the Lord, Jesus Christ. When we commit our lives to Christ, we are making a conscious decision to honor Him with our body, souls and spirit. Life and life eternal are found in Jesus, for He alone is capable of saving.

Although you have life and life more abundantly through Christ Jesus, He never promised that life here on earth would be easy. However, despite all the curveballs that life may bring, your ability to remain faithful in Him, lends to a great reward.

Today, I want to encourage you to remain faithful and place all trust in Jesus. Yes, life will get hard, and close friends and family may turn away, but through it all, the Lord promised that He would never leave you nor forsake you. In Jesus, there is great gain.

Dear Heavenly Father

Lord God, in Jesus' name, Father, I thank You for helping me to remain faithful in You. Father, I thank You for showing me Your love and allowing me to honor You in the same manner. Lord, in Jesus' name, I ask for Your peace to shower me all the days of my life. In Your Son Jesus' name, I pray, amen.

Faithfulness

Day 64

You are Restored, In Jesus' Name

"I will restore your judges as at the first, And your counselors as at the beginning. Afterward you shall be called the city of righteousness, the faithful city." - Isaiah 1:26

ೞ

Surely, God is in the season of Restoration. God desires to restore you to the original version in which He created You. You will be restored. You will be made whole; your family's legacy will be renewed in Jesus' name. No longer will you be labeled desolate or barren, for you will be fruitful and multiply. You will have life and life more abundantly. The Lord God desires for you to be whole and complete in Him. You will lack nothing in Jesus' name, amen.

If you didn't know, Heaven is banking on you. God and a host of Angels are rooting for you. You will be restored and made whole in Jesus' name. You've been faithful, you've been steadfast, you've been praying, and you've been sitting at the feet of Jesus. Therefore, God is opening the flood gates of Heaven over you. You are about to walk into a season of an abundance of breakthrough and healing in Jesus' name. Continue to honor the Father and continue to desire His will.

Dear Heavenly Father

Lord God, in Jesus' name Father, I honor You with my life. Lord, I thank You for establishing me in Your truth. Father, I ask that You steady my feet in Your will, in Your Son Jesus' name, I pray, amen.

Day 65
To Reverence Him

"He commanded them, saying, 'Thus you shall act in the fear of the Lord, faithfully and with a loyal heart:" - 2 Chronicles 19:9

☙

Proverbs 9:10 tells us that the fear of 'the Lord is the beginning of wisdom.' When the Bible uses terms such as 'fear of the Lord', it does not mean that we are afraid of Him – as in terrified, but rather we reverence Him. To fear the Lord is to reverence Him, to honor Him, and to seek to please Him.

When fearing the Lord or reverencing Him, you have an innate response to wanting to please Him. This does not mean that you'll never mess up or fall out of alignment with God – we can only pray that you won't. Your natural desires to please Him will cause You to be connected to the Father with no regard to the number of times you mess up or how perfect your walk is.

God is looking for faithful servants who will honor Him with their whole hearts. Remember, David was considered a faithful servant and a man after God's own heart – though he messed up numerous times. This is not a get-away-with-sin pass. This is an encouragement to honor God and to reverence Him, although you've sinned and fallen short of His glory.

Dear Heavenly Father

Lord God, I thank You for purifying my heart in Jesus' name. Lord, I pray that You baptize me in Your Spirit, in Jesus' name. Father create in me a heart that longs after You. In Jesus' name, I pray, amen.

You are Redeemed

"I will betroth you to Me in faithfulness, and you shall know the Lord." – Hosea 2:20

ೂ

There will be a time when the Lord redeems you. When God redeems you, you will be complete and lack nothing. Everything you've ever done and will do, is leading to the moment when you will be reconciled with the Father.

It's an honor and privilege to be able to have an intimate relationship with the Father, our Creator. It's even more breathtaking to know that the Creator of this entire universe desires to have a relationship with you. The type of relationship the Father wishes to have with you is an eternal union that leads to an everlasting life. Yes, your life here on earth is only a fraction of time in which God has invested in you.

There's a scripture that tells us that eyes have not seen nor have ears heard the plans that God has prepared for those who love Him (*See 1 Cor. 2:9*). Surely, God has marvelous plans for you, both here on earth and in Heaven. It's a great joy to know that regardless of what takes place in our lives, God has so much glory in store for us. As a redeemed child of the Almighty, walk with great courage and confidence, knowing that God has great things in store for you.

Dear Heavenly Father

Lord God, I ask that You open my eyes to see the marvelous things that You have for me. Lord, in Jesus' name Father, keep my feet walking steadfastly in You, amen.

Day 67
Will You?

> "Only fear the Lord, and serve Him in truth with all your heart; for consider what great things He has done for you." - 1 Samuel 12:24

ଔ

One thing that God is looking for is someone who will honor Him with their whole heart. God is not interested in those who give Him lip service – those who say, 'Lord, I am for You,' but their actions are not lining up with what they speak. Will you honor and serve God with your whole heart?

Think about this, would you stay in a relationship with someone who continuously gives you empty promises, or, someone who is not 'practicing what they're preaching?' That's the same way God is. Every relationship should contain individuals who are putting in some good ol' work.

So, how about it? Will you give God your 'yes' and work towards having an intentional, intimate and personal relationship with God? Will you? The perfect thing about saying 'yes' to Christ is that you don't have to be perfect; simply give it your best and try. Make an effort to spend quality time with Jesus, make an effort to submit your life to Him. When God sees your effort, He'll take it from there. God will bring the increase in your life and give you an increased desire for Him.

Dear Heavenly Father

Holy Spirit, I ask that You help me as I strive to spend quality time with You. Father, I ask that You keep my mind from wandering and keep my heart focused on You. Lord, thank You for increasing my desires for You. In Jesus' name, I pray, amen.

Faithfulness

Day 68

Do not Faint

"For if we died with Him, we shall also live with Him. If we endure, we shall also reign with Him. If we deny Him, He also will deny us. If we are faithless, He remains faithful; He cannot deny Himself." – 2 Timothy 2:11-13

☙

2 Timothy 2:13 says, 'if we are faithless, He remains faithful; {God} cannot deny Himself.' Your lack of faith does not change God's stance concerning what He said or what He desires to do through you nor for you.

If you choose to never believe in God again, God still exists, and He remains faithful. Your lack of faith does not scare God; in fact, He charges us to have faith in what is not seen. This is called; blind faith, crazy faith, undoubting faith, wild faith, bold faith and Now Faith. It takes the strength and power of God to walk in faith because it's easy believing in what we can see or even perceive. However, it takes God's grace to move forth in faith in the things that are unseen.

I believe there are somethings that you're believing God for, and the enemy is trying to cause you to lose your faith, and he's trying to cause you to doubt Jesus. I want to encourage you to hold on. The Word of God says that 'if *you* endure, *you* shall reign *and reap* with Him' emphasis added. Your *Now Faith* will produce a harvest. Do not faint.

Dear Heavenly Father

Lord, thank You for showing me that my strength to endure and walk with bold faith, is found in You. Father, thank You for fighting all my battles. Lord, help me to seek You more. In Jesus' name, I pray, amen.

My Sweet Savior • 90 Day Devotional

Day 69

The Greatest of them All

"And it shall be that if you earnestly obey My commandments which I command you today, to love the Lord your God and serve Him with all your heart and with all your soul, then I will give *you* the rain for your land in its season, the early rain and the latter rain, that you may gather in your grain, your new wine, and your oil." - Deuteronomy 11:13-14

ଔ

It's a given; the Lord wants us to obey His commandments and honor Him with our whole hearts. For in doing so, we shall reap the rewards of life.

If we were to scale the entire Bible and search for all of God's commandments, we'd search for days. In addition, the moment we find a new commandment, chances are we'd either break the ones we've already found or forgotten what they were. Luckily for us, the greatest commandment sums up all of God's mandates. LOVE. Jesus is Love, and God tells us to abide in Him. The Lord knows that if we abide in Jesus (love), if we put our trust in Jesus (love), and desire to walk in Jesus (love), then everything else God requires will be fulfilled. The way of life is found in Jesus. In Jesus, there is an abundance of life.

Dear Heavenly Father

Lord, Thank You for showing me that You are Love and in You, are the fulfillment and riches of life. Lord, help me to walk in love. Father, help me to love myself as well as my neighbors. Father in Jesus' name, I thank You, amen.

Faithfulness

Day 70

New Name

"I thank Christ Jesus our Lord who has enabled me, because He counted me faithful, putting me into the ministry, although I was formerly a blasphemer, a persecutor, and an insolent man." – 1 Timothy 1:12-13

ൠ

The titles you once wore means nothing to God. Those labels that you've placed on yourself and what others have placed on you is null and void in God's hands.

The moment you committed your life to Christ was the moment Jesus washed your sins away. The moment you repented was when Christ forgave you. You are made new in Jesus' name. The Word of God tells us that there is no condemnation for those who are in Christ Jesus *(see Romans 8:1)*. As a woman after God's own heart who is not walking in your own desires nor in the 'flesh,' walk in freedom knowing that God chose you. No longer allow fleeting thoughts or the judgments of this world keep you from walking in the fullness of God. God has renamed you Beloved. Walk in your newness.

Dear Heavenly Father

Lord God, in Jesus' name, I am free. Father, I have placed my undying and unwavering trust in You. Lord, I have committed my life to You. Father, I have desired Your ways, and because of such, You've given me a new name. Lord, You've washed my sins away and gave me life. So, Lord, in Jesus' name, Father, I thank You. In Jesus' name, I pray, amen.

Words for You

Sis, at this moment, a scripture that comes to mind is found in 2 Corinthians 5:17, which states, "Therefore, if anyone *is* in Christ, *he is* a new creation; old things have passed away; behold, all things have become new."

As a woman of God who desires and seeks after Jesus, know that in Christ, you're a new creation. One of the gifts of dedicating your life to Christ, and placing your faith in Him, is that everything concerning you is made new. Regardless of what comes your way, know that you are a Kingdom Woman. Your faith must be in Heaven. Your faith must be in Jesus. I'm not saying that your journey will be comfortable, you'll have some rocky roads. However, your trust and confidence in Christ will ensure you'll have a joyous ride, one that's filled with tons of wisdom and knowledge.

I want to encourage you to live, laugh, and learn. In life, we're charged to live and to live abundantly in Christ Jesus. Also, scripture encourages us to laugh for 'a merry heart does good like medicine' - Proverbs 17:22. Not to mention, the Lord tells us that if anyone lacks wisdom, to ask and it shall be given, liberally. - James 1:5

Above all else, my hope and prayer for you are that through your journey, you find joy and peace in Christ Jesus.

Dear Heavenly Father

Lord God, I pray for my sister. Father, I pray that she finds hope, faith, and peace in You through Christ Jesus. Father, comfort her and shower her with Your love. Father, I ask that as she continues to seek You, that You take her from glory to glory, as she goes from faith to faith. In Your Son Jesus' name, I pray, amen.

Quiet Time

Prayer Request

Reflective Notes | Reflective Questions

Scriptures

Gentleness

Day 71

You are His Warrior

"Therefore, as the elect of God, holy and beloved, put on tender mercies, kindness, humility, meekness, longsuffering" – Colossians 3:12

ଓଃ

If you have not heard, God is a gentle Father. Everything about God yells 'Gentleman.' He is patient, kind, and loving towards all. His Spirit is sweet and quiet yet holds might and authority. It's no wonder that as children of God, He calls us in the same manner.

Very often, when we hear the terms tender mercies, kindness, humility, meekness, longsuffering, and I'd go even further to say, submission, we react somewhat grudgingly. A grudging reaction is often as a result of these terms appearing as if they fall into the same category as; weak, pushover, or doormat. However, this is far from the truth. When God tells us to put on tender mercies mixed with some gentleness, it's because we're strong and pack a powerful punch. Yes, it's true; only God's most resilient warriors can walk boldly in His gentleness, humility, longsuffering, and the like.

It takes the power of the Holy Spirit to experience life at its fullest and yet walk with a gentle and loving spirit. Today, choose to allow God's Spirit to empower you to walk in love and all gentleness.

Dear Heavenly Father

Lord God, Father, I thank You for giving me Your Holy Spirit, which enables me to walk in Love, humility, and gentleness. Father, I ask that Your Holy Spirit continues to empower me for good, as I seek to live and do Your will. In Your Son, Jesus' name, I pray, amen.

Gentleness

Day 72

Gentle Spirit

"Walk in wisdom toward those who are outside, redeeming the time. Let your speech always be with grace, seasoned with salt, that you may know how you ought to answer each one." – Colossians 4:5-6

ఴ

Colossians 4:5 said it beautifully. 'Walk in wisdom toward those who are outside.' The word '*outside*' means those who are outside of the faith, those who are non-believers, and even those who are not on the same 'plateau' as you, spiritually.

Contrary to popular belief, we are to show love and light to all, including non-believers. There's a false misconception that insinuates, God's children are not supposed to share love, compassion, and even grace to those who are outside of the faith. This misconception is far from the truth. Jesus' purpose was to seek (find, look for, and being compelled) and save (redeem, love, and draw closer) the lost. If Jesus is called to the lost, with the intentions of redeeming and saving them, then we're called to do the same.

With our gentle spirit and the Lord's wisdom, we can be the salt of this world to preserve humanity while leading them to Jesus.

Dear Heavenly Father

Lord, I thank You for showing me how to be the salt of this world. Father, I thank You for granting me provision to love on and to lead Your souls back to You through my loving and gentle spirit. In Your Son Jesus' name, I pray, amen.

Day 73
The Source of Life

"A soft answer turns away wrath, but a harsh word stirs up anger." - Proverbs 15:1

ಜ

Your tongue and your words are powerful. With very few words, you have the power to be a lethal weapon or bring about resurrection. For the Word of God says, life and death are in the power of the tongue. - Proverbs 18:21. Just as God was able to speak everything into existence, we have that same authority.

Scriptures like; Proverbs 23:7, Luke 6:45, Proverbs 18:21 and even Proverbs 15:1, shows us that the authority God has given us is stored up in our belief. As we believe in our hearts, our words activates our belief, that is why the Lord says, as a man thinks, so is he and out of the abundance of a man's heart, he will speak.

The Lord is actively cautioning His children to use their words for good and not for evil. To use their words to bring forth life and fruit.

As you continue your day and even your walk with Christ, think about your words before speaking. A great question to ask yourself is, *'is my response or my comment bringing glory to Christ? Is what I'm saying drawing souls closer to Him, or will it be a stumbling block?'*

Dear Heavenly Father

Lord God, I ask that You guide my words and my thought process. Father, help me to be mindful of my words, actions and my belief. Lord, I desire to draw souls closer to You, so Holy Spirit lead me. In Jesus' name, I pray, amen.

Gentleness

Day 74

Where is your Beauty?

"Let your gentleness be known to all men. The Lord is at hand." - Philippians 4:5

೧೮

The questions I wish to place on the table are; Where is your beauty? What's the foundation of your identity? What draws others towards you? Where is your attraction?

Now, before you answer these question, try not to confuse beauty and identity with your appearance nor your status quo. Your beauty and identity are both found in Christ. When Christ looks at you and examines you, He will never consider your appearance. The things of this world does not interest Him. The Lord is only interested in the content and matters of your heart. When the Lord examines you, some of the many things He is checking is; your ability to be pliable in His hands, your willingness to honor Him, and your desire to share His love within this world.

God cares about these things. The Lord is looking for a generation who desires to seek His will, walk-in His precepts, love and honor Him and His children. Will that be you?

Dear Heavenly Father

Lord, thank You for molding my heart and image in You. Father, I ask that You continue to mold me, and allow my love and reverence for You to permeate through me. Father, I desire to walk in Your godly beauty, one that represents You while leading others to Your glory. In Jesus' name, I pray, amen.

The Foundation of Love

"You shall not hate your brother in your heart. You shall surely rebuke your neighbor, and not bear sin because of him. You shall not take vengeance, nor bear any grudge against the children of your people, but you shall love your neighbor as yourself: I am the Lord." - Leviticus 19:17-18

ख

The Old Testament is just as valuable, valid, and useful as the New Testament. The entire Bible is created on the premise of LOVE. John 4:7 tells us that God is love, and then it proceeds to tells us that God manifested Himself in love, in the form of His only begotten Son, Jesus.

When it comes to godly love, it corrects others with the intention of either protecting them or leading them on a proper path. When the Word of God tells us that we should not hate our brother, followed by instructions of rebuke, we must honor the primary facet. The key point is that when we correct or rebuke others, we must have our hearts planted in loving them. God honors a pure heart whose motives are rooted in love. When your motives are rooted in love, it magnifies the Father even more.

Dear Heavenly Father

Lord, I ask that You continue to check my heart and motives. Father, test me to ensure that my heart is pure before You. Lord, if I ever walk out of the abundance of my flesh and emotions, Father, I ask that You lead me back into Your heart of LOVE. In Jesus' name, I pray, amen.

Gentleness

Day 76

Let Compassion Lead

"Thus says the Lord of hosts: Execute true justice, show mercy and compassion everyone to his brother. Do not oppress the widow or the fatherless, The alien or the poor. Let none of you plan evil in his heart Against his brother." – Zechariah 7:9-10 9

ଓ

There's a difference between being led by your emotions and flesh and being led by the Holy Spirit. It's essential to know what's driving you.

Have you ever heard the saying, 'don't make decisions when you're angry?' Well, the reason is that 'anger' is an emotional feeling. When making decisions when you're angry or feeling other strong emotions, for that matter, you tend to act according to the way you feel. For instance, if someone annoys you, you're quick to cut them off and even disregard their feelings due to their actions and the result of whatever situation is at hand.

However, you may feel one way concerning an individual or situation while God is leading you to handle it differently. At times, our emotions can cause us to miss God's intended will and lesson. Therefore, incline your ear to the Spirit of the Lord and allow compassion to lead you in love and understanding.

Dear Heavenly Father

Lord, I ask that You help me to lean on You for all my understanding. Father, keep my feet from seeking my own will and way. In your Son Jesus' name, Lord, guide me, amen

Day 77

To Judge Righteously

"Therefore let us not judge one another anymore, but rather resolve this, not to put a stumbling block or a cause to fall in our brother's way." Romans 14:13

☙

In the Bible, there are two forms of judging. The first one is mentioned in Romans 14:13. The second pertains to a righteous judgment, which is mentioned in John 7:24. Just to be clear, God wants us to judge one another. However, it must stem from a righteous stance. To judge righteously is to have a heart posture fixed on Jesus, with the intent of helping someone. Righteous judgment does not put someone on blast nor condemn them.

To know the difference between the two, first and foremost, read the scriptures. Secondly, examine your heart and the situation at hand. Before speaking on something, consider this, is what you're about to say offensive? If so, are you speaking in love, or are you speaking in anger, frustration, or even jealousy? If you're speaking in love, ask the Holy Spirit to guide your words. Assure that person that you have good motives. On the contrary, if you're not about to speak in love, wait until you have a clear conscience and can deliver your message with good intentions.

This is merely a blueprint of questions and suggestions you can incorporate to avoid speaking and operating in condemning judgment.

Dear Heavenly Father

Lord, I thank You for helping me to walk and speak in love. Father, I know that my words have the power of life and death. Therefore, help me to speak life in all situations. In Jesus' name, I pray, amen.

Gentleness

Day 78

Purpose in Repetition

"Therefore, as we have opportunity, let us do good to all, especially to those who are of the household of faith." – Galatians 6:10

☙

It's often stated that when something is referenced more than once, we should pay attention to it. Though we should pay attention to the entire Bible, when something is referenced multiple times, our antennas should be up.

As born-again Believers of Jesus Christ, in addition to showing love, grace, kindness, and mercy to those who are of the faith, we should also remember to show the same grace and love to those who are outside of the faith. It should be noted that the reason why this verse and many alike are referenced is, because, just like today, numerous believers failed to show grace and even do good to those who are outside of the faith. This breaks God's heart.

God's will is for all men to be saved and come into the knowledge of salvation through Jesus Christ. However, we, as believers, have a crucial part to play. Showing love and the same grace to all men will advance the Kingdom of Heaven. Just like we attract more bees with honey, we attract more believers to Jesus with love, grace, and compassion.

Dear Heavenly Father

Lord, I Thank You for giving me the wisdom of knowing how to treat all men according to Your glory and will. Lord God, I ask that You grant me more opportunities to show the same love and compassion to all men so that I may lead them to You. In Jesus' name, I pray, amen.

Day 79
The Full Body of Christ

"Let brotherly love continue. Do not forget to entertain strangers, for by so doing some have unwittingly entertained angels." – Hebrews 13:1-2

ଔ

As the Body of Christ, we extend far beyond the walls of the church. We're an extension of Christ, and just as Christ spread His love towards us, we also extend our love towards the world, far beyond the church walls.

Romans 11:16-17 states that if the first-fruit is holy, the lump is also holy; it proceeds by telling us that if the root is holy, so are the branches. Finally, Romans 11:17 ends off by stating that we were once 'wild olive' trees not belonging to that tree. However, we were '*grafted*' in and became partakers of that root. The 'Root' of discussion is the Kingdom of Heaven. This scripture is telling us that we were once 'wild' beings not belonging in the Kingdom of Heaven. However, Jesus saw fit to graft us in by His Blood. Therefore, just as Jesus grafted us in, He can fuse anyone by His love and His Blood.

Today, walk with a gentle spirit by meditating on Jesus' Word, knowing that His love and salvation is for 'whosoever will.'

Dear Heavenly Father

Lord, I love You. I adore You. So, Father, I magnify Your Name, and I lift Your name. Father, I pray for the ENTIRE Body of Christ. Father, I pray that You lead all Your sons and daughters back to You. In Jesus' name, I pray, amen.

Gentleness

Day 80

Life Producing Words

"Pleasant words are like a honeycomb, sweetness to the soul and health to the bones." – Proverbs 16:24

☙

In all things, remember that your gentle spirit can produce healing. By the Holy Spirit, you have the power to bring forth life in someone's life and even their situation.

Have you ever encountered someone who prophetically spoke encouraging words to you? Often when we receive a word of encouragement, our entire day is shifted for the better. We tend to walk with newfound confidence knowing that God hears you, and He cares about you, as you should. God cares about you without measures.

Therefore, I want to challenge you. Everyday make it a priority to speak life and encourage yourself. In addition, ask the Lord to guide you and lead you to others whom you can bless with words of encouragement, that's inspired by the Holy Spirit. Just imagine, the world we live in would be filled with more love and compassion if everyone could band together to uplift one another.

Dear Heavenly Father

Father, In Jesus' name, Lord, I ask that You help me to be an encouragement and light to others. Lord, I know Your Words have healing and can bring forth life into dead situations. Therefore, Lord, I ask that You plant Your Words in my mouth as I seek to share Your love and wisdom. In Jesus' name, I pray, amen.

Words for You

It's almost like I hear the sweet precious Voice of our Savior whispering 1 Peter 3:4. He's reminding me to tell you that the hidden Person of your heart, which is the Holy Spirit in you, is transforming you into an incorruptible beauty that consists of a gentle and quiet spirit. God is pleased with you, for you are precious in the sight of God. The Lord loves you undoubtedly, for you are the apple of His eye, and He calls you beloved.

Sis, if you cry, let it be tears of joy. Walk in the boldness of Jesus knowing that before the Lord formed you in your mother's womb, He knew you. Also, the Lord **pre**-sanctified you and ordained you. To be pre-sanctified means that God cleansed you by the Blood of Jesus, knowing that you will have faults and mistakes.

Lastly, before we close out for today, I want to leave you with another reminder. Gentleness, humility, and boldness always work together. Being gentle and walking in humility does not negate the fact that you are a bold virtuous woman of God. It takes a bold woman of God to walk in both gentleness and humility. After all, Jesus was bold and authoritative yet humble among all men.

Dear Heavenly Father

Lord, I thank You for blessing Your daughter. Father, I ask that You grant her the peace knowing that she is Your daughter, and that she's called by You. Father, I ask that You grace her with Your gentle and loving Spirit. Father, all who enters her path will experience a taste of Your love. In Jesus' name, protect, and keep her, amen.

Quiet Time

Prayer Request

| **Reflective Notes** | **Reflective Questions** |

Scriptures

Self-Control

My Sweet Savior • 90 Day Devotional

Day 81

Inhale, Exhale

"But also for this very reason, giving all diligence, add to your faith virtue, to virtue knowledge, to knowledge self-control, to self-control perseverance, to perseverance godliness, to godliness brotherly kindness, and to brotherly kindness love." – 2 Peter 1:5-7

ଓଃ

In this walk with Christ, we're called to fight the good fight of faith. This fight of faith should be exercised in all areas in life, such as; purity, spiritual warfare, test and tribulations, family, friends, work, and even school – just to name a few. However, at times, for us as women of God, fighting the good fight of faith can prove to be challenging.

During our everyday tasks and responsibilities, while living for Jesus, we may run close to the edge with our cups nearly empty. We tend to find ourselves drained, hopeless, helpless, confused, and frustrated. During those moments, remember to breathe. Even the best of us tend to lose it from time to time. However, God is not only concerned about a loss. God is watching your handle. How are you handling things when you feel burned out and close to the edge? In all things, remember to breathe, knowing that God has your life and your situation cradled in the palm of His hands. He is actively working on your behalf. So, as you inhale God's peace, exhale confusion and keep breathing.

Dear Heavenly Father
Help me to breathe. In Jesus' name, I pray, amen.

Self-Control

Day 82

Fruit of Life

"Death and life are in the power of the tongue, and those who love it will eat its fruit." – Proverbs 18:21

☙

Good Morning! The Word of God tells us that we'll know the tree by its fruit. What you believe and meditate on is considered the seed. The production or manifestation is the fruit. Therefore, you'll receive an inclination of what's in one's heart by their words and actions.

The Fruit of Life will bear record that the seeds you've planted in your soul were cultivated by the Word, tended to with compassion, and watered by love. Due to us living in a fallen world, it'll take much intentionality on your part to desire and eat of the Fruit of Life. To eat of the Fruit of Life is to love and desire the will of God. Though, I believe 1 Corinthians 13:4 - 10 described the Fruit of Life perfectly. The Fruit of Life is LOVE. GOD is love.

To obtain the Fruit of Life is to be a child of God, walking and trusting in His love.

Dear Heavenly Father

Lord, In Jesus' name, I thank You for giving me the seed of Love. Lord, I desire to eat the Fruit of Life. So, Father, thank You for showing me how-to walk with You so that I may produce Your Fruit. In Jesus' name, I pray, amen.

My Sweet Savior • 90 Day Devotional

Day 83

Virtuous Women of God

"He who is slow to anger is better than the mighty, and he who rules his spirit than he who takes a city." – Proverbs 16:32

ಛ

There is something so profound about the quietest person in the room. Though this person is not necessarily shy, instead, she's bold, observant, and at peace.

Women of God, as you surround yourself with others within this world, remember who you are. You are a beautiful, resilient, strong, and phenomenal woman of God. You own every single lane where God places you. You understand that there's no need for strife, nor is there a need to get angry and sweat out your eyebrows nor your edges. You know the power of your presence and the power of your virtue; therefore, you protect it at all costs. And to top it all off, you stand boldly on Proverbs 31:30 because you understand that charm is deceitful, and beauty is passing. However, as a woman of God, a virtuous woman of God who fears the Lord - all of Heaven rejoices over you. Daughter of the Most High God, stand tall in the Lord.

Dear Heavenly Father

Lord God, in Jesus' name, I pray that You continue to open my eyes to the wonder of Your Spirit that is within me. Help me to continue to walk tall and confidently, knowing that I am Your daughter and You favor me. In Jesus' name, I pray, amen.

Self-Control

Day 84

The power of Your Purity

"No temptation has overtaken you except such as is common to man; but God is faithful, who will not allow you to be tempted beyond what you are able, but with the temptation will also make the way of escape, that you may be able to bear it." – 1 Corinthians 10:13

☙

When people hear the word 'purity,' their first thoughts tend to be abstinence. However, purity is more significant than just abstaining from sex. Purity deals with the state of your wholeness.

The Word of God tells us that no temptation has overtaken you except such that is common to all. Simply put, any temptation you may face, know that others have faced the same form of enticements. The Lord proceeds to tells us that He remains faithful because He continuously gives you a way of escape.

Your way of escape comes in the form of renewing your mind in the Holy Spirit. It takes intentionality and knowledge to know that you are redeemed, and whom the Son sets free is free indeed. Whatever temptation or challenging situation you're facing today, know that Jesus has redeemed you by His Blood. Now, it's time to cherish the purity of your redemption. Renew your mind with the Word of God.

Dear Heavenly Father

Jesus, I thank You for Your Blood. Thank You for redeeming me and establishing me so that I may remain free in my body, soul, and spirit. In Your Great name, I pray, amen.

You have the Power

"Whoever has no rule over his own spirit Is like a city broken down, without walls." – Proverbs 25:28

☙

You are NOT like a city broken down without walls. You are a child of God who knows the power of self-control and walks in the full authority that Christ has given you.

The term, 'walking in authority' is to walk boldly in humility. To be in authority is to be humble enough to know how to treat others with love and kindness, yet bold enough to walk confidently in your identity. Someone who walks authoritatively knows that being a tyrant trying to gain influence and power, only proves weakness. When you walk in authority, you're confident that your strength and self-control come from Jesus. As the Lord is the increaser and supplier of all, He increases you with more power and influence as you're faithful with the first and last thing He has given you.

Dear Heavenly Father

Lord, In Jesus' name, I ask that You continue to establish me in Your peace. Help me to be steadfast and confident in whom You've called me to be. Lord, I recognize that my love, power, and authority is Your Spirit strengthening and developing me. So, Father, In Jesus' name, I ask that You continue to do Your work. In Jesus' name, I pray, amen.

Self-Control

Day 86

Fear Not

"For God has not given us a spirit of fear, but of power and of love and of a sound mind." – 2 Timothy 1:7

☙

In Joel 2:28, the Lord prophesied through Joel that He would pour out His Spirit on all flesh. 1 John 4:7 tells us that God is Love. 1 John 4:18 proceeds by stating, 'there is no fear in love {because} perfect love casts out fear.'

Ironically, many believers struggle and are bound by fear; fear of the unknown, fear of being obedient, fear of being confident, fear of the Devil, and fear of missing the Lord, to name a few. The list of crippling fears that are over many of the Lord's children is incredibly long.

As a child of God, you must get a hold of the truth that Jesus conquered your every doubt. In Him, fear does not exist. However, this does not mean that fear or doubt is entirely void in us. On the contrary, this means that in Christ, you have surety in His love, knowing that He will never leave you nor forsake you. If God has spoken a promise over your life, hold fast to faith. If God said it, then surely it shall come to pass. Whenever fear and doubt tries to creep in, remind yourself that your God is greater, bigger, and more faithful than those lies.

Dear Heavenly Father

Father, I thank You for establishing Your perfect love within me. Lord, help me as I place my trust and hope in You. Father, Your Word says that You will never leave me nor forsake me. So, Lord, in Your promises, I will trust. In Jesus' name, I pray, amen.

Day 87

You can Fight this

"Therefore, let us not sleep, as others do, but let us watch and be sober." – 1 Thessalonians 5:6

ೞ

1 Thessalonians 5:6 reminds me of the Garden of Gethsemane scene in Matthew 26:36-56. In this scene, Jesus went for prayer and told His disciples to keep watch. However, they were stricken with a deep heaviness of sleep. When Jesus saw that they were sleeping, rather than staying awake, praying, and keeping watch, He became upset and disappointed with them. – *If you have never read this, please do so, it will bless your life.*

Surprisingly, in comparison to the Garden of Gethsemane scene, nothing has changed. God is continuously cautioning His sons and daughters to remain 'woke' and aware of the times and seasons that we're in as individuals, a body, a nation, and the world. God is calling every believer to partake in His portion of intercession. He wills for us to deny our flesh, our desires, and the cravings of this world so that we can surrender to Him and walk in His will.

We must know and understand that God does not want His children to become paralyzed by spiritual sleep paralysis. The enemy desires to place a numbing agent around the hearts and minds of God's children. However, you fight back with the renewing of your mind.

Dear Heavenly Father

Lord, teach me to renew my mind. Father, establish my heart in the precepts of Your Word. Lord, I ask for a spiritual boost of energy and desire to remain cognizant of Your will and ways. In Jesus' name, I pray, amen.

Self-Control

Day 88

With Wisdom and Understanding

"So then, my beloved brethren, let every man be swift to hear, slow to speak, slow to wrath." – James 1:19

☙

In all your getting, get understanding. – Proverbs 4:7

The communication and understanding barrier that abounds stem from not asking nor seeking wisdom and understanding. However, the Word of God encourages us to seek after wisdom. The rationale for such encouragement is because wisdom and understanding breeds to life.

When one possesses such attributes, it aligns them with the knowledge of what's happening in their lives and in the lives of others. With your newfound revelation of God's will, compassion will soon override fear, apprehension, doubt, and even anger. Wisdom and understanding are God's gifts to all His children, which means love is the foundation. With love being the foundation of God's gifts, obtaining them gives you the grace to honor James 1:19. After all, loves covers a multitude of sins.

Dear Heavenly Father

Lord, You said that if anyone lacks wisdom that they should ask, and You'd give it. So, Lord, in Jesus' name, I ask for more wisdom and understanding. Father, I desire to know your will and love your Children. Lord, I know that in loving and understanding Your will and your children, it will prevent wrath. Your love of wisdom and understanding is the breeding ground for brotherly love. In Jesus' name, I pray, amen.

Day 89

It is Possible

"For the grace of God that brings salvation has appeared to all men, teaching us that, denying ungodliness and worldly lusts, we should live soberly, righteously, and godly in the present age" – Titus 2:11-12

☙

It is possible. You can live soberly, righteously, and wholly in the Lord. You can abstain from sex if you desire to. You can honor the Lord your God with your body, mind, and spirit. You can grow and develop in the love of Christ. You can become a virtuous woman of God. You can walk boldly, while pushing past fear and objection.

You will become a ray of life for all who watch you. Your family and generations to come will be blessed because of your obedience. You will be healed spiritually. Your feet will remain planted in the Lord, and you will be like a tree planted in rivers of waters, one which brings forth fruit in its due season.

Every morning, I want you to remind yourself of this truth. When life tries to knock you down, remember that you are an overcomer. You can overcome all things through Christ Jesus. It is possible because His Spirit lives within You. The Lord has sent His Holy Spirit to guide you and lead you into all truths.

Dear Heavenly Father

Lord, I thank You for building me strong and powerfully. Lord, I thank You for planting in me the seed of an overcomer's spirit. Father, by Your hands and by Your Spirit, I will remain steadfast, unshakable, and unmovable. Jesus, I thank You for Your Blood, amen.

Self-Control

Day 90

What does this mean? Renew

"And do not be conformed to this world, but be transformed by the renewing of your mind, that you may prove what is that good and acceptable and perfect will of God." – Romans 12:2

ೀ

To renew your mind, what is it? What does renewing your mind in the Lord look like to you?

Well, we have finally made it to Day 90. I'm proud of you for keeping the pace. Sure, you may have missed a day here and there, jumped around, and read what pertained to you. However, none of that matters. What matters the most is that you've pressed on and are still pressing on.

As daughters of the King, God calls us to be sanctified and set apart in Him. To be sanctified is to be washed and made new in His image. To be set apart is to abstain from the ways of this world, not conforming to its image and the standard that it has given you.

Sis, you are royalty. From this day forward, your life will never be the same. Your walk and posture will magnify the King. How do I know? Because this is the perfect will of God for your life. God will for you is to know Him more with each passing day. Therefore, His Holy Spirit will see to it that you continuously walk with Him.

Dear Heavenly Father

Lord, I thank You for choosing me. Father, ever since You came into my life, I've been a changed woman for the better. Lord, I smile differently. Father, I talk differently, and most importantly, I shine from inside out, and it's all because of Your Glory and Love. So, Father, in Jesus' name, I thank You, amen.

Words for You

Sis, when you see the word 'self-control' listed as one of the fruit of the spirit, know that it yields to a righteous submission. FYI, a righteous submission is not a curse word! When it comes to the things of the Lord, submit simply means, yielding to the Holy Spirit and allowing the Lord to be Lord over your life. We're granted free will in Christ Jesus, so you're capable of walking as you wish – though the Lord urges us to choose life.

Choosing Life is to honor the Word of God while knowing and understanding that we're not perfect. We all fall short of the Glory of God. However, we're not exempt from striving to be the best version that God intended us to be. Life is not a sprint, and the race is neither given to the swift, nor the strongest, but rather the one who endures to the end.

The Lord knows that multiple times in our lives, we'll mess up and fall short, so He graces us. The grace the Lord has given you lies in your endurance, self-control, or in other words, your ability to walk in righteous submission, which is yielding to the Holy Spirit.

Today, I want to encourage you to endure. I know it's easier said than done. For this reason, a tip towards endurance is knowing the Word of God, His promises, and keeping faith and hope that if God said it, then surely it shall come to pass.

Dear Heavenly Father

Lord, I ask that You continue to grant Your daughter, peace, and assurance, knowing that You have given her Your Spirit of endurance. Lord, I ask that You continue to keep her feet from failing. Father be her peace amid her chaos. Father, in Jesus' name, I thank You for loving Your daughter, amen.

Quiet Time

Prayer Request

Reflective Notes | Reflective Questions

Scriptures

My Sweet Savior

Closing

So, here you are, vulnerable and naked before the Lord. It seems scary, and at times you're unsure if you can keep this up. You don't know if you have what it takes to continue to submit to Jesus. At times, you question if you have what it takes to remain consistent with reading your Word and having an intimate and quiet time with Him.

However, the Lord is saying; *it's okay*. While He wants you to read every day, what matters to Him the most is your heart and your soul. He cares about the content of your heart, so after you close the pages of this Devotional, He'll continue to do the great work in You. At times, it'll feel as if you're being pruned without measure. You may even feel scared and alone. And not to mention, you'll question your purpose and your very existence. In all things, remember what we've talked about.

The focus of this Devotional was to show evidence that God has never left you, He's doing a great work in you, and you have what it takes to be a great steward of His Word and will. Everything you need to be confident in this walk with Christ is already within you. The moment you took your first step towards salvation and living for Jesus, Christ planted His Spirit within you. You'll always have the Holy Spirit with you. Your Helper is positioned to strengthen and reveal all truths to you.

I know, at times, it'll be hard and challenging to incline your ear to the Lord; therefore, before we leave, I want to bless you with some practical tips that you can implement daily.

Five Practical Tips

1. Smile

Life has a way of trying to knock you down. Therefore, no matter what, remember that you are a child of the Most High King. In all things, smile, knowing that you are called according to His purpose. Smile, knowing that trouble does not last always. Smile, knowing that the Lord loves you, and He has chosen you.

2. Breathe

As you inhale, inhale the peace and love of God. As you exhale, exhale anxiety, confusion, and the chaos of this world. The Lord loves you, and there is nothing too hard for Him. He will make a way for you. He has gone before you. Therefore, breathe, remain at peace, knowing that God is a good Father, and His plans for you are for good and not of evil.

3. Live

While you have the opportunity, seize the moment to live. Make time to explore and fulfill your wildest dreams. God has given you life; therefore, you have permission to live on purpose.

4. Laugh

Proverbs 17:22 tells us that a merry heart does good, *like* medicine, but a broken spirit dries the bones. Therefore, at every given moment, remember to laugh. The Lord has come to bring you life and life more abundantly. Laugh, for laughter brings pure joy to the soul.

5. Be Bold

Proverbs 28:1 says that the righteous are as bold as a lion. May you walk in the boldness that the Lord has given you. May you never shrink due to fear nor doubt. May you rise in faith knowing that if God is before you, then **NO ONE** can be against you!

Ending Prayer

Dear Heavenly Father,

Lord, I thank You for drenching me in Your presence. Father, I ask that You draw me closer in Your arms. Lord, I thank You for loving me unconditionally while removing all conditions. Father, I thank You for forming me into a marvelous, and virtuous women for Your glory. Father, You existed before I was formed, and I know that You always will. So, Father, thank You for considering me and for walking with me. You are my forever friend. And God, I just love You with my entire soul. In Your precious Son Jesus' name, I bless You. Amen.

Salvation Prayer

Dear Heavenly Father,

In Jesus' name, I repent of my sins. I ask that You forgive my sins and trespasses. Lord, I also ask that You help me acknowledge You in all that I do. Jesus, I ask that You come into my heart and be Lord over my life. Father, Your Word in Romans 10:9-10 says, 'that if I confess with my mouth the Lord Jesus and believe in my heart that YOU have raised Him from the dead, then I will be saved.' So, Father, with my mouth I confess and with my heart I believe that Jesus died on the cross for my sins and that You raised Him from the dead so that I may live. In Jesus' name, I pray, Amen.

Thank you for rescuing me from the powers of darkness. You have given me victory and dominion over my enemies. For this and much more, I give thanks to Jesus Christ, my Lord and Savior. Amen.

Since you said this prayer and have dedicated your life to Christ (or back) by faith, you are saved! I would love to hear of your great news and would love to help keep you accountable by inviting you to join our Discipleship program. Register at:

www.RiseMinistry.org/Discipleship

Books by Armani White

You're More Than Enough
Owning your Purpose

♦

My Sweet Savior
'90 Day Devotional'
Building an Intimate Relationship with Jesus

♦

Prayer Tool

Courses

"*My Sweet Savior 90 Day Devotional – Building an Intimate Relationship with Jesus*" is paired with Rise Ministry, Inc.'s Discipleship Program. If you desire to build an intimate relationship with Jesus and to know Him more, it's highly recommended that you join our online **Discipleship Program**.

To find out more about the program and to register, log on to www.RiseMinistry.org/Discipleship.

Online Book Writing Course – No More delay, Publish your book NOW! Visit us at: www.RiseMinistry.org/PublishNow